THE HEINEMANN
ACCOUNTANCY AND ADMINISTRATION SERIES

General Editor: J. BATTY, D.COM.(S.A.), M.COM.(DUNELM), A.C.W.A., M.B.I.M.

Fundamentals of Accounting 1

FUNDAMENTALS OF ACCOUNTING

Volume 1: Fundamentals and Preparation of Accounts
Volume 2: Partnership and Other Special Accounts
Volume 3: Company Accounts

FUNDAMENTALS
OF ACCOUNTING

VOLUME 1

Fundamentals and Preparation
of Accounts

by

JOHN KELLOCK, C.A.

Prizeman, Institute of
Chartered Accountants of Scotland

HEINEMANN : LONDON

William Heinemann Ltd

15 Queen St, Mayfair, London W1X 8BE

LONDON   MELBOURNE   TORONTO
JOHANNESBURG   AUCKLAND

434   91040   6   (hardback)

434   91043   0   (limp)

*Set in 10/12 pt. Monotype Times New Roman, printed by photolithography
and bound in Great Britain at The Pitman Press, Bath*

Editor's Foreword

The *Heinemann Accountancy and Administration Series* is intended to fill a gap in the literature that caters for accountants, company secretaries, and similar professional people who are engaged in giving a vital information service to management. Due recognition is given to the fact that there are two distinct bodies of readers: those who aspire to professional status—the students—and others who are already managing and/or serving management. Whenever possible the books are written with this distinction in mind.

Financial accounting examinations require that students should be able to understand the methods and then put them into practice with speed and efficiency. There is no short cut to success—practice and still more practice, is the only way to reach the necessary degree of proficiency.

John Kellock is a very able and experienced lecturer who has developed a consistently successful method of teaching. In this book he takes the student through the many stages involved and, provided the student understands the principles and can apply them, he should have no difficulty in reaching the exacting standards required in the intermediate stages of the accountancy examinations set by professional bodies.

At no stage in the history of accountancy have examination standards been so high. A study of the Pass Lists (or should they be called 'Failure Lists') will show that a large proportion of candidates fail to reach the level required. Inevitably, Accounting presents one of the major barriers.

Students cannot reach the necessary standard in Accounting without determination and hard work. However, the method of teaching can play a considerable part in helping the student to build up the necessary knowledge and proficiency. For this reason I am pleased to welcome this new book to the Series. I am sure it will prove a worthy companion to the books already published.

J. BATTY

Preface

This is Volume 1 of a series of three books covering the fundamentals of accounting. This modular approach to the subject has been adopted so that students may study the texts by progressive stages and in this way a full coverage of the areas required for the elementary and intermediate stages of the accountancy examinations of the various professional and non-professional bodies is provided. Alternatively each book may be regarded as being quite self-contained within the areas indicated by the title.

The aim of publishing the three volumes is to consider the fundamentals of financial accounting in a simple, concise, and logical manner so that students may assimilate the principles of accounting in a relatively clear and understandable form.

In Volume 1 I have dealt with the basic principles of double-entry accounting together with several topics which frequently occur in accountancy examinations at an elementary stage. Each topic covered has been illustrated with examples which I have used in my own lectures. The questions have been selected to clarify the points discussed in each chapter and to demonstrate the form of presentation best suited to the solution of these problems.

The scope of this volume is not limited to any single examination syllabus but covers the elementary stages of accountancy examinations set by the various professional and non-professional bodies.

I wish to acknowledge the permission granted by the following bodies to incorporate questions in this book which were set by their examining boards:

Institute of Chartered Accountants of Scotland	(C.A.)
Institute of Chartered Accountants in England and Wales	(C.A. E. & W.)
Association of Certified Accountants	(A.C.C.A.)
Institute of Cost and Works Accountants	(I.C.W.A.)
Chartered Institute of Secretaries	(C.I.S.)
Corporation of Secretaries	(C. of S.)
Society of Commerical Accountants	(Com. A.)
London Chamber of Commerce	(L. Ch. of C.)

I acknowledge permission from Kalamazoo Ltd. to reproduce one of their accounting forms.

My thanks are also due to Dr. J. Batty for his encouragement and assistance while I was writing these books and to Mrs. I. Thomson, Dip.Com., who read through the manuscript and offered valuable observations and suggestions which have been incorporated in the final form of the books.

I express very great gratitude to my wife who, although she had many other commitments to fulfil, found time not only to prepare the typescript but also to assist me in the secretarial matters associated with it.

Finally, in token of my respect and affection I dedicate this work to my Mother and Father.

JOHN KELLOCK

Contents

Editor's Foreword		v
Preface		vii

1 INTRODUCTION TO THE PRINCIPLES OF DOUBLE ENTRY ACCOUNTING
1.1	Introduction	1
1.2	Requirement of accounting records	1
1.3	Balance sheet	3
1.4	Double entry accounting	4
1.5	Ledger	7
1.6	Day books	9
1.7	Cash book	13
1.8	Journal	18
1.9	Trial balance	20

2 PREPARATION OF TRADING AND PROFIT AND LOSS ACCOUNTS AND BALANCE SHEET
2.1	Introduction	29
2.2	Trading account and profit and loss accounts	29
2.3	Treatment of balances on asset and liability accounts	32
2.4	Accrued and prepaid charges	37
2.5	Accrued and prepaid income	40
2.6	Bad debts	41
2.7	Provision for discount allowed	44
2.8	Provision for discount received	45
2.9	Classification of accounts in the profit and loss account	46

3 BANK RECONCILIATION STATEMENT; PETTY CASH BOOK; CORRECTION OF ERRORS
3.1	Bank reconciliation statement	56
3.2	Petty cash book	60
3.3	Correction of errors	65

4 DEPRECIATION
4.1	The necessity for providing depreciation	75
4.2	Factors to be taken into consideration in determining the depreciation charge	76

4.3 Methods of depreciation   77
4.4 Plant register   88
4.5 Accounting entries for the purchase and sale of fixed assets   88

5 CAPITAL AND REVENUE EXPENDITURE
5.1 Capital expenditure   101
5.2 Revenue expenditure   101
5.3 Necessity to distinguish between capital and revenue expenditure 102

6 BILLS OF EXCHANGE AND CHEQUES
6.1 Introduction   109
6.2 Definition of a bill of exchange   109
6.3 Bill books   113
6.4 Promissory notes and cheques   113
6.5 Contingent liability   115
6.6 Accounting entries to record bills of exchange   115

7 SELF-BALANCING LEDGERS AND CONTROL ACCOUNTS
7.1 The necessity for self-balancing ledgers and control accounts   127
7.2 Advantages of self-balancing ledgers   127
7.3 Construction of a purchases ledger total account   128
7.4 Construction of a sales ledger total account   129
7.5 Purchases and sales ledger control accounts   131
7.6 Sub-division of purchases and sales ledgers   134

8 MANUFACTURING ACCOUNTS
8.1 Introduction   141
8.2 Manufacturing costs   141

9 INCOMPLETE RECORDS
9.1 Introduction   150
9.2 Single entry accounting system   150
9.3 Single entry accounting system with the introduction of a cash
     book   157

Index   176

1 Introduction to the Principles of Double Entry Accounting

1.1 INTRODUCTION

Accounting is a term which may be described as the science, or if preferred, the art of identifying, recording, measuring, and reporting of financial information. In broad terms it is an information-gathering system which records and measures economic events which take place in business. By analysing and interpreting this information those in control of business organizations are able to base their decisions on realistic accounting data rather than on intuition. Since the measurement of profit or loss is an involved process where large amounts of capital are invested in costly assets such as land and buildings, plant and machinery, stock and debtors it is essential that accurate accounting information is available and personnel are trained in the compilation and interpretation of such data.

The whole study of Accounting may be divided into two parts:

(*a*) The mechanics of recording and presenting financial data. This aspect principally deals with procedural matters.
(*b*) The interpretation and reporting of financial results in business organizations.

This book is primarily intended to discuss and examine the various techniques which are used to record financial information. A section has been included, however, to illustrate the methods adopted to interpret accounting statements and the reporting of financial information to directors, shareholders, and others in control of business activities.

1.2 REQUIREMENT OF ACCOUNTING RECORDS

While it is possible to conduct a small business without a highly complex accounting system, there is still a need for accounting records if only in a restricted and incomplete form. As a business develops and expansion takes place the necessity for additional financial information increases. The accounting system must always remain flexible to enable it to keep pace with the changes and development occurring in the business itself. It is quite absurd to have advanced scientific techniques and modern machinery in operation in the factory and an outdated and inadequate accounting system operating in the office. It is important that as great an emphasis is placed on the accounting function in the business as that on the technical and selling aspects. To justify the paramount importance of the accounting function in a business, it is imperative that the output of the accounting system supplies the quantitative information required by managers, at all levels, in a form to enable them to make the correct economic decisions. It is obvious and indeed only natural that the accounting system must be tailored to meet the needs of the business and not the business arranged to suit a rigid and ill-conceived accounting system.

1.21 INFORMATION PROVIDED BY ACCOUNTING RECORDS

Basically the business accounting records should provide the following information:

(a) The amounts due to suppliers of goods and services and the amount due by customers for goods supplied to them or work carried out on their behalf.
(b) The amount of revenue expenses incurred by the business, e.g. wages, rent, rates, electricity.
(c) The amount of cash in hand and cash at the bank.
(d) The total purchases and sales.
(e) The amount of assets owned by the business, e.g. land and buildings, motor cars, plant, and equipment.

1.22 FINANCIAL STATEMENTS PREPARED FROM ACCOUNTING INFORMATION

From this information the following financial statements may be extracted:

(a) A Trading and Profit and Loss Account showing the overall profitability or otherwise of the business operations.
(b) A Balance Sheet listing the assets owned by the business and the liabilities owed by the business.
(c) Cost statements showing the profit or loss earned by each department or section of the business.

(*d*) Comparative financial statements indicating variances in revenue expenditure and income in different accounting periods.

The above data is basic in form and is common to almost every class of commercial enterprise, illustrating the type and form of accounting information which can be derived from most accounting records. Even in this simplified and general form sufficient control information can be provided to measure the effectiveness of management and to assist in business decision making. More sophisticated accounting techniques can be and are applied to assist management in attaining the policy objectives of the business but these are discussed in a later chapter in this book.

1.3 BALANCE SHEET

One of the most important financial accounting statements is the Balance Sheet. Its importance stems from the fact that it reveals the overall financial position of a business and discloses the assets of the business, the liabilities, and the owner's capital. Indeed, one of the principal reasons for recording accounting entries is to enable such a statement to be prepared. As will be mentioned later, the Balance Sheet is closely linked with the Trading and Profit and Loss Accounts and collectively form the Final Accounts of a business. Below is an example of a Balance Sheet drawn up in a simple form to illustrate the principles underlying its compilation.

Balance Sheet as at 31 December

Capital		£5,000	Assets:	
Liabilities:			Motor Car	£1,000
Creditors	£2,000		Stock	3,500
Loan	1,000		Debtors	3,000
		3,000	Cash	500
		£8,000		£8,000

The Balance Sheet is compiled from three main items—Assets, Liabilities, and Capital, which are defined as follows:

Assets: Broadly speaking assets are things of value usually of a tangible nature such as property, plant, motor cars, stock.

Liabilities: Liabilities are amounts owed by a business such as sums due to creditors, bank overdrafts, loans, mortgages.

Capital: Capital is the excess of assets over liabilities and is considered the owner's equity.

The foregoing Balance Sheet has been drawn up at 31 December from the balances appearing on the relevant accounts at that date. Unlike the Trading and Profit and Loss Accounts the Balance Sheet is not a ledger account but a statement of assets and liabilities.

1.31   ASSETS = LIABILITIES + CAPITAL

From a study of the Balance Sheet it will be seen that Assets = Liabilities + Capital.

As will be observed in the next section this equation must always be true because the assets of a business must be equal to the liabilities and the owner's capital since each transaction has a two-fold effect in its accounting treatment.

The equation may, of course, be expressed in another way:

Assets − Liabilities = Capital.

1.4   DOUBLE ENTRY ACCOUNTING

One of the fundamental principles of accounting theory is that two items are affected by each transaction. To facilitate the recording of transactions entries are written in accounts. An account is opened for each aspect of every transaction and the amount of the transaction is posted to the debit side of one account and to the credit of another thus observing the double entry principle. Before a transaction can be considered to be correctly recorded a debit entry and a credit entry have to be made in the accounts affected by the transaction. This is the reason why accounts are two-sided, thus accommodating both debit and credit entries. The debit entries are recorded on the left-hand side of the account and the credit entries on the right-hand side.

At this stage following the double entry concept of accounting it will be appreciated that after entering a series of transactions the total debit entries in these accounts must be equal to the total credit entries. Since the Balance Sheet is a list of balances (a balance being the difference of debit and credit entries in an account) grouped into assets (debit balances) and liabilities and capital (credit balances) the totals of both sides of the Balance Sheet must be the same.

The following example illustrates this important accounting principle:

George Smith commences business on 1 January with capital of £1,000 in cash. This opening transaction will affect the Capital Account and the Cash Account and will be shown in this way:

Dr.   *Capital Account*   **Cr.**

| | Jan. 1   Cash | £1,000 |

Cash Account

Jan. 1   Capital   £1,000 |

If a Balance Sheet is drawn up on 1 January after recording this transaction it will appear thus:

Balance Sheet as at 1 January

| Capital | £1,000 | Asset   Cash | £1,000 |

On 2 January George Smith purchases a motor car in cash for £500. This transaction will affect both the Cash Account since cash is reduced by £500 and the Motor Car Account to record the acquisition of the car.

Dr.   *Motor Car Account*   **Cr.**

| Cash | £500 | |

Cash Account

| Balance | £1,000 | Motor Car | £500 |

George Smith decides on 2 January to open a Bank Account and agrees to transfer £300 from his cash to the Bank Account. This transaction is recorded in the following accounts.

Dr.   *Bank Account*   **Cr.**

| Cash | £300 | |

Cash Account

| Balance | £500 | Bank | £300 |

Note: The opening balance on the Cash Account is calculated:

Capital	£1,000
Less: Payment for car	500
	£500

On 2 January George Smith received a loan of £600 from Arthur Brown to assist in the expansion of his business. This amount was paid by cheque which would affect the Bank Account and the Loan Account in the name of Arthur Brown:

Dr. *Bank Account* **Cr.**
Balance £300
Loan—Arthur Brown 600

Loan Account—Arthur Brown
Bank £600

If a Balance Sheet is drawn up after these transactions have been recorded
it would appear thus:

Balance Sheet as at 2 January

Capital	£1,000	Assets:	
Liabilities:		Motor Car	£500
Loan—Arthur Brown	600	Bank	900
		Cash	200
	£1,600		£1,600

1.41 ACCOUNTING PROCEDURE FOR POSTING TRANSACTIONS TO
ASSET AND LIABILITY ACCOUNT

By studying the previous example it is possible to enumerate certain rules
for posting entries to asset and liability accounts. It is important at this stage
to appreciate the procedures adopted for recording transactions in account
form. These may be summarized as follows:

(*a*) If any asset account is increased the increase is recorded as a debit
in the asset account.
(*b*) Alternatively if any asset account is decreased the decrease is recorded
as a credit.
(*c*) If any liability account or owner's capital account is increased the
increase is recorded as a credit in the relevant liability account or
owner's capital account.
(*d*) Alternatively if any liability account or owner's capital account is
decreased the decrease is recorded as a debit.

Although asset accounts are represented by debit balances they do not
normally appear on the left-hand side of the Balance Sheet, as would appear
to be the logical position for them, but are shown on the right-hand side.
This presentation has been adopted by convention rather than standard
accounting practice. The liability and owner's capital accounts, of course,
appear on the opposite side of the Balance Sheet to the asset accounts.

1.5 LEDGER

The Ledger is one of the principal books in any accounting system. In the ledger is a record of accounts of customers, suppliers, and also those of an impersonal nature such as plant and machinery, rent and rates, electricity. From scrutiny of the ledger accounts it is possible to ascertain how much is owed by customers, the amount due to suppliers, the total expenses incurred during a particular period, and the assets and liabilities of the business. Although it is quite practicable to retain these accounts within one ledger it is not theoretically correct since ledger accounts can be classified into main groups and consequently separate ledgers should be kept to record the various groups of accounts. Ledger Accounts are divided in the following categories:

Personal Accounts recorded in Sales and Purchases Ledger
Nominal Accounts recorded in the Impersonal Ledger
Real Accounts recorded in the Impersonal Ledger which also may be referred to as the Nominal Ledger.

1.51 PERSONAL ACCOUNTS

Personal Accounts are those accounts in which are recorded details of financial transactions with suppliers and customers. Any balance appearing on the debit side of a personal account indicates that there is a sum due to the business and a credit balance signifies a sum due to be paid to a customer or creditor.

1.52 NOMINAL ACCOUNTS

Nominal Accounts are used to record the loans, expenses, and gains of the business. Debit balances on nominal accounts relate to expenses and losses while credit balances indicate income or profit.

1.53 REAL ACCOUNTS

Real Accounts represent assets. Examples of real accounts are Motor Vehicles, Plant and Machinery, Furniture and Fittings, Property, all of which have debit balances. In real accounts assets purchased are debited and assets sold credited.

8 FUNDAMENTALS AND PREPARATION OF ACCOUNTS

Elementary Illustration of Writing Up Ledger Accounts

The following example is intended to illustrate the use of ledger accounts to record business matters.

Question

Jan. 1 A. Green commenced business and introduced £200 in cash, as capital.
    2 Purchases are made for cash   £50
    3 Cash sales amount to   £40
    4 Wages paid in cash   £10

You are required to write up the relevant ledger accounts to record the above.

Suggested Solution:

Folio 1 — *Cash Account*

Dr.   Cr.

Date	Particulars	Folio	Amount	Date	Particulars	Folio	Amount
Jan. 1	Capital	2	£200	Jan. 2	Purchases	3	£50
3	Sales	4	40	4	Wages	5	10

Folio 2 — *Capital Account*

				Jan. 1	Cash	1	£200

Folio 3 — *Purchases Account*

Jan. 2	Cash	1	£50

Folio 4 — *Sales Account*

				Jan. 3	Cash	1	£40

Folio 5 — *Wages Account*

Jan. 4	Cash	1	£10

Notes

(a) The ledger account is divided into two sections—debit and credit. The ruling for each side is identical giving the date, particulars, folio of account to which posted, and amount of each entry.

(b) It will be noted that each entry has been recorded in the ledger twice—in one account as a debit entry and in another as a credit. This, of course, conforms to the fundamental double entry principle which states that every transaction has a two-fold aspect which must be recorded.

(c) The folio column is a means of referencing the postings between different books and accounts. From this short example it is quite apparent to which account each posting is made without reference to folios but in practice the correct and systematic use of folios is essential due to the numerous and sometimes complex postings made in the accounting system.

(d) In this example owing to the small number of ledger accounts opened, separate ledgers have not been used to classify the accounts.

(e) In many accounting text books the words 'To' and 'By' are used to preface debit and credit entries respectively in the ledger. Since these prefixes are now being discontinued in modern accounting systems they have been omitted throughout this book.

(f) The ledger accounts in this example have not been balanced. The technique of balancing ledger accounts is first of all to add both sides of the account and subtract the two totals.

The difference between these totals is inserted as a balance on the side of the account with the smaller total and both sides then again added. The total on both sides of the account should now agree. The balance is brought down as a balance on the opposite side of the ledger account. For example, if the cash account had been balanced in this illustration it would have appeared thus:

Dr.			*Cash Account*				Cr.
Jan. 1	Capital	2	£200	Jan. 2	Purchases	3	£50
3	Sales	4	40	4	Wages	5	10
					Balance c/d		180
			£240				£240
5	Balance b/d		£180				

1.6 DAY BOOKS

1.61 SALES AND SALES RETURNS DAY BOOKS

When credit sales are numerous it is convenient to use a memorandum book to list particulars of those transactions. This book is called a Sales Day Book in which are entered details of goods sold on credit similar to those included on the invoice sent to the customer. Each entry in the Sales Day Book is posted to the debit of the customer's account in the Sales Ledger while the credit to the Sales Account is only posted periodically, usually monthly when the Sales Day Book is totalled. This reduces the number of postings to the latter account.

If credit notes are frequently sent to customers in respect of allowances on goods returned then it will be advisable to enter these credit notes in a Sales Returns Day Book before posting the items to the ledger accounts. The customer's accounts in the Sales Ledger will be credited with the amount of the credit note and the total of the Sales Returns Book posted periodically to the Sales Returns Account.

1.62 PURCHASES AND PURCHASES RETURNS DAY BOOK

Since most businesses purchase goods on credit it is customary to open a Purchases Day Book for the recording of particulars contained in invoices received from suppliers. Not only does this book serve as a posting medium to the ledgers but it acts as a reference book giving details of date, price, type, name of supplier, and cost of goods purchased on credit. The amount of each credit purchase is posted to the credit of the supplier's account in the Purchases Ledger and the total of the Purchases Day Book posted at regular intervals to the Purchases Account.

In the same way if credit notes are numerous then it is convenient to list them in a Purchases Returns Day Book. The amount appearing in the credit note is posted to the debit of each supplier's account and the total of the Returns Day Book posted to the credit of Purchases Returns Account.

The following question illustrates the method used to record transactions in the day books and thereafter posting them to the ledger accounts.

Question

Record the following transactions in the Purchases and Sales Day Books and post to the ledger. No folios are required.

    Jan. 1 Bought on credit from J. White timber £50
            Bought on credit from J. White ironmongery £25
         3 Sold on credit to J. Thomson cabinets £30
            Sold on credit to J. Thomson tables £40
         4 Returned goods bought from J. White—timber sub-standard £10
         5 J. Thomson returned one table damaged £15

Suggested Solution:

PURCHASES DAY BOOK

Date	Particulars	Folio	Amount	Amount
Jan. 1	J. White Timber Ironmongery		£50 £25 ——	 £75 —— £75

SALES DAY BOOK

Date	Particulars	Folio	Amount	Amount
Jan. 3	J. Thomson Cabinets Tables		£30 £40 ——	 £70 —— £70

PURCHASES RETURNS BOOK

Date	Particulars	Folio	Amount	Amount
Jan. 4	J. White— Timber returned as sub-standard			£10

SALES RETURNS BOOK

Date	Particulars	Folio	Amount	Amount
Jan. 5	J. Thomson— One table returned—damaged			£15

Note: The Day Books do not form part of the double entry system but are purely memoranda books in which total purchases, sales, and returns are recorded.

PURCHASES LEDGER
J. White Account

Dr.							Cr.
Jan. 4	Returns		£10	Jan. 1	Purchases		£75

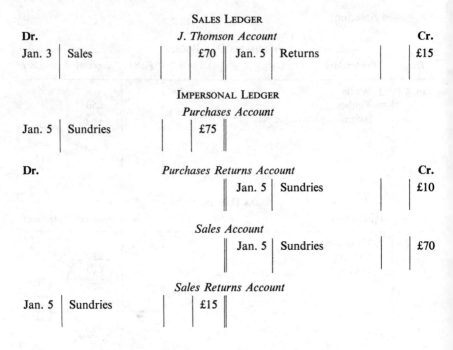

SALES LEDGER

Dr. *J. Thomson Account* **Cr.**

| Jan. 3 | Sales | £70 | Jan. 5 | Returns | £15 |

IMPERSONAL LEDGER
Purchases Account

| Jan. 5 | Sundries | £75 |

Dr. *Purchases Returns Account* **Cr.**

| | | Jan. 5 | Sundries | £10 |

Sales Account

| | | Jan. 5 | Sundries | £70 |

Sales Returns Account

| Jan. 5 | Sundries | £15 |

1.63 TRADE DISCOUNT

It is necessary to note at this stage the treatment of trade discount in accounting records. Trade discount is an allowance given by the seller of goods to the buyer which is deducted from the gross amount of the sale in the invoice sent to the buyer. On entering the amount in the day book the gross amount is shown in an inner column and the trade discount deducted therefrom. The net amount is then posted to the personal account of the buyer in the sales ledger. On no account is trade discount shown as an amount in the ledger. The following example illustrates this procedure.

SALES DAY BOOK

Date	Particulars	Folio	Amount	Amount
Jan. 1	R. Thomson			
	10 Desks @ £10 each		£100	
	Less: 20% Trade Discount		20	
			——	£80

Only £80 will be posted to R. Thomson's account in the Sales Ledger. Similar information will be recorded in R. Thomson's Purchases Day Book.

1.64 COLUMNAR DAY BOOKS

It is quite common to find in the Day Books additional information to that shown in the previous example. Many businesses which deal in more than one product find it convenient to analyse their purchases and sales in the Day Books thus enabling sales and purchases to be classified under appropriate headings. This form of analysis allows the owner of the business to calculate the profitability of each class of merchandise in which he is trading; whereas under the original form of Day Book this would not be possible without further analysis being made.

For example, a trader who deals in office equipment may rule the Purchases Day Book thus:

Date	Particulars	Invoice No.	Folio	Total	Type-writers	Office Furniture	Adding Machines
Jan. 1	Typewriter Company	1	PL 2	£55	£55		
3	W. S. Smith Ltd.	2	PL 6	£100		£100	
5	A. B. Addo	3	PL 9	£92			£92

The postings to the ledger will be made in the usual way. Similar type rulings can be used for the Sales Day Book and Returns Books if the same form of analysis is desired.

1.7 CASH BOOK

The Cash Book which is a book of original entry is used to record receipts and payments by cash or cheque. It performs a similar function to a ledger and is ruled in a similar form with debit and credit sides. Several rulings are adopted in practice to suit the requirement of each business. Some of the more important types of Cash Book rulings are discussed below.

In effect both the cash account and bank account are incorporated in this one book with columns headed for each account on both the debit and credit sides. The cash book in this form is known as a two-column cash book. While this system is commonly used in practice it is still possible to keep the cash and bank accounts separate if this is found more convenient. Since the cash book is essentially composed of two ledger accounts the principles of double entry are observed when entries are recorded in it and the following rules should be observed:

Dr. Cash Book (Cash Column) with all cash received.
Cash Book (Bank Column) with all amounts received by the bank or paid into the bank.

    Cr. Cash Book (Cash Column) with all expenditure paid in cash.
        Cash Book (Bank Column) with all expenditure paid by cheque or by
        the bank direct (e.g. banker's order, etc.)

Contra Entries

    This type of entry arises when a transfer occurs between the cash column
and the bank column both of which are contained in the cash book.

    If an amount of cash is transferred to the bank the entries are as follows:

    Dr. Cash Book (Bank Column) with the amount of cash lodged in bank.
    Cr. Cash Book (Cash Column).

    On the other hand if an amount is withdrawn from the bank for office
cash the entries are:

    Dr. Cash Book (Cash Column) with amount of cash withdrawn from
        bank.
    Cr. Cash Book (Bank Column).

    As the double entry is taking place within the cash book it is referenced
(C) in the folio column.

    This question illustrates the use of the two-column cash books.

Question

    You are required to record the undernoted transactions in the books of
G. Rowan on the following bases:

    (*a*) Using a cash account and a bank account.
    (*b*) Using a two-column cash book.

After recording the entries balance the cash and bank accounts and cash
book bringing down the balance on the last day of the month. Ledger
postings are not required.

Jan. 1 Capital introduced in cash by G. Rowan £500.
      2 G. Rowan opened a bank account and lodged £200 out of the cash intro-
          duced as capital.
      3 Cash purchases £50.
      7 Cash sales £60.
    12 Paid for purchases by cheque £75.
    18 Cash sales paid into the bank £35.
    25 Sundry expenses paid in cash £10.
    30 Paid wages by cheque £40.
    31 Paid electricity by cheque £15.

Suggested Solution:

(*a*) Using cash and bank accounts.

Dr.   *Cash Account*   **Cr.**

Jan. 1	Capital	£500	Jan. 2	Bank	£200
7	Sales	60	3	Purchases	50
			25	Sundry Expenses	10
			31	Balance c/d	300
		£560			£560
Feb. 1	Balance b/d	£300			

Dr.   *Bank Account*   **Cr.**

Jan. 2	Cash	£200	Jan. 12	Purchases	£75
18	Sales	35	30	Wages	40
			31	Electricity	15
				Balance c/d	105
		£235			£235
Feb. 1	Balance b/d	£105			

(*b*) Using two-column cash book.

CASH BOOK

Dr.   **Cr.**

Date	Details	Folio	Cash	Bank	Date	Details	Folio	Cash	Bank
Jan. 1	Capital		£500		Jan. 2	Bank	(C)	£200	
2	Cash	(C)		£200	3	Purchases		50	
7	Sales		60		12	Purchases			£75
18	Sales			35	25	Sundry Expenses		10	
					30	Wages			40
					31	Electricity			15
						Balance c/d		300	105
			£560	£235				£560	£235
Feb. 1	Balance b/d		£300	£105					

Note: By comparing the two solutions it is quite apparent that the cash book contains the same information as recorded in the separate cash and bank accounts.

1.71 THREE-COLUMN CASH BOOK

A further development to the two-column cash book is the addition of one column on both the debit and credit sides to accommodate discount allowed to customers and discount received from suppliers. This form of cash book is referred to as the three-column cash book. The cash and bank columns are written up in an identical manner as in the two-column cash book. The discount columns are purely memoranda columns for recording the allowances for discount allowed and received and do not form part of the double entry system. The total of the discount allowed column is posted to the debit of Discount Allowed Account in the Impersonal Ledger while the total of the discount received column is posted to the credit of Discount Received Account in the same ledger.

Question

This question illustrates the use of the three-column cash book. Enter the following particulars in a three-column cash book and bring down the balances at the end of the period:

Jan. 1 Tom Lee commenced business with cash £500.
    5 Paid into Bank £100.
  10 Purchased goods for cheque £70.
  12 Received cheque for £25 from B. Ford in settlement of his account of £26.
  15 Paid sundry expenses in cash £5.
  18 Sent R. Smith cheque in settlement of his account of £60, less 5% discount.
  25 Cash Sales £25.
  27 Sent cheque for £88 to W. Jones being allowed £2 discount.
  31 Paid wages by cheque £30.

Suggested Solution:

Cash Book

Dr.

Date	Details	Folio	Discount Allowed	Cash	Bank
Jan. 1	Capital	(c)		£500	£100
5	Cash				25
12	B. Ford		£1		
25	Sales			25	
31	Balance c/d				120
			£1	£525	£245
Feb. 1	Balance b/d			£420	

Cr.

Date	Details	Folio	Discount Received	Cash	Bank
Jan. 5	Bank	(c)		£100	£70
10	Purchases				
15	Sundry Expenses			5	
18	R. Smith		£3		57
27	W. Jones		2		88
31	Wages				30
	Balance c/d			420	
			£5	£525	£245
Feb. 1	Balance b/d				£120

Notes: (a) The credit balance at end on the bank account indicates that this is overdrawn to the extent of £120.

(b) The discount columns are not balanced in the cash book but are posted as separate amounts to the Impersonal Ledger.

(c) When posting the cash received to B. Ford's Account the follow-narrative and amount will appear on the credit side of his personal account:

Jan. 12   Bank and Discount   £26

The following narrative and amount will appear on the debit side of R. Smith's account:

Jan. 18   Bank and Discount   £60

1.73 COLUMNAR CASH BOOKS

In many businesses the three-column cash book is not adequate to deal with the number of cash and bank transactions and additional columns are necessary to cope with the required analyses. Extra columns for wages, travelling expenses, trade expenses, rent, rates, insurance, and other items of expenditure may be introduced so that the number of postings to these accounts will be minimized by only posting the total of the columns, say monthly, to the nominal accounts in the impersonal ledger.

1.8 JOURNAL

There is a general principle in accounting that one of the aspects of each transaction, either debit or credit, must be recorded in a book of original entry. The books of original entry are the Cash Book, Purchases and Sales Day Books, and the Returns Books. While most business transactions are recorded in one of these books before being posted to the Ledger there are some which cannot be entered in this way. Transfers from one ledger account to another, correction of errors in ledger accounts, opening and closing entries, purchases and sales of fixed assets where the day book is not used for such transactions, are all examples of items which do not appear in a book of prime entry. In order that this important accounting rule can be observed another book is introduced into the accounting system which is known as the Journal. Although the Journal is primarily reserved for record-ing those entries previously referred to, it is possible, while not practical, to journalize every transaction in accounting since the composition of a journal entry is only to indicate which account is to be debited and which account credited followed by a narrative explaining the nature of the transaction. For example, if the following business transaction is journalized—On 1 January H. Scott bought on credit from W. Jones goods for resale to the value of £100—the journal will read:

Date	Particulars		Folio	Amount	Amount
Jan. 1	Purchases	Dr.	IL 1	£100	
	To W. Jones		PL 1		£100
	Being goods purchased on credit				

The above illustration is known as a journal entry and indicates that the Purchases Account is to be debited with £100 and a similar sum is to be credited in the Supplier's Account. The narrative at the end of the journal entry merely explains the transaction. This form of transaction would not, of course, be journalized since the original entry would be made in the Purchases Day Book but is only shown at this stage to illustrate the fact that it is possible to journalize each trading transaction.

The Journal is ruled in a similar fashion to the Day Books and in some ways performs a similar function to those books. Indeed quite often the Day Books are referred to as Journals. The Journal, however, does not form part of the double entry accounting system but acts as a posting medium for special accounting entries. The following question is an example of a transaction which would be recorded initially in journal form.

Question

The Trading Company purchased on credit from the Business Machines Company a typewriter for £75 on 1 January.

Suggested Solution:

JOURNAL

Folio 1

Date	Particulars		Folio	Amount	Amount
Jan. 1	Office Equipment	Dr.	IL 1	£75	
	To Business Machines Co.		PL 1		£75
	Being purchase of a typewriter on credit				

PURCHASES LEDGER

Dr.	*Folio 1*	*Business Machines Co. Account*			Cr.
		Jan. 1	Office Equipment	J1	£75

IMPERSONAL LEDGER

Dr.	*Folio 1*	*Office Equipment Account*		Cr.
Jan. 1	Business Machines Company	J1	£75	

Note: There is usually no need to total the Journal as each entry stands on its own but it may be useful to add both sides of a journal entry which involves several items to ensure that both totals agree.

The various uses to which the Journal can be put are discussed in a later chapter in this book.

1.9 TRIAL BALANCE

A Trial Balance is simply a list of all the balances appearing in the ledger accounts and cash book at any given time. The balances so extracted are arranged in two columns headed debit and credit and both columns when totalled should be equal in amount. This is the main feature of a Trial Balance which is intended to prove the arithmetical accuracy of the books. If the total appearing in the debit column does not agree with that in the credit this would signify that the double entry principle has not been correctly applied in recording the trading transactions. This deduction can be confidently made due to the fact that every transaction requires two entries in the books of account, viz. a debit and a credit, therefore it follows that the total debits must be equal to the total credits and on balancing the accounts the total debit balances should equal the total of credit balances.

This technique is extensively used in practice and it only fails to reveal errors of a type which would not cause a disagreement in the trial balance. Those errors are errors of omission, commission, compensating, and principle, which are discussed in some detail later.

The following question illustrates the type of transactions which take place in businesss and their treatment in the accounting records.

Question

You are required to enter the following transactions in the correct books of original entry and post to the ledgers and thereafter extract a Trial Balance as at 31 January.

Jan.	1 C. Brown commences in business by paying into bank	£1,000
	2 Withdrew by cheque for office cash	100
	3 Bought goods on credit from R. Smith £50 and	
	D. Jones £250.	
	4 Sold good on credit to B. Finch £70 and	
	R. Gold £55.	
	6 Returned goods bought on credit from R. Smith received a credit	
	note from him	10
	7 Paid D. Jones cheque for amount of his account *less* £12 discount.	
	9 Allowed R. Gold a deduction from his account of £5 in respect	
	of goods which arrived at his warehouse damaged.	
	11 Paid in cash wages	25
	12 Cash Sales amounted to	120
	13 Purchased goods for cheque	200
	15 Purchased by cheque motor van	500
	17 Received cheque from R. Gold *less* £2 discount	
	20 Sold goods on credit to P. Smart	125
	22 Sent R. Smith a cheque to settle his account	
	25 B. Finch sent a cheque in full settlement of his account	70
	29 Purchased goods on credit from T. West	63
	30 Paid wages in cash	25
	31 Paid electricity by cheque	15

Suggested Solution:

Folio 1

Dr.   CASH BOOK   **Cr.**

		Folio	Discount Allowed	Cash	Bank			Folio	Discount Received	Cash	Bank
Jan. 1	Capital	IL1		£100	1,000	Jan. 2	Cash	(C)			£100
2	Bank	(C)		120		7	D. Jones	PL2	12	25	238
12	Sales	IL3				11	Wages	IL2			200
17	R. Gold	SL2	2		48	13	Purchases	IL4			500
25	B. Finch	SL1			70	15	Motor Van	IL5			40
						22	R. Smith	PL1		25	
						30	Wages	IL2		170	15
						31	Electricity	IL6			25
							Balances c/d				
			£2	£220	£1,118				£12	£220	£1,118
			Folio 9						Folio 10		
Feb. 1	Balances b/d			£170	£25						

IMPERSONAL LEDGER

Dr.   **Cr.**

Folio 1   *Capital Account*

| | | | | Jan. 1 | Bank | CB1 | £1,000 |

Folio 2   *Wages Account*

Jan. 11	Cash	CB1	£25
30	,,	CB1	25
			£50

Folio 3   *Sales Account*

				Jan. 12	Cash	CB1	£120
				31	Sundries	SDB1	250
							£370

Folio 4   *Purchases Account*

Jan. 13	Bank	CB1	£200
31	Sundries	PDB1	363
			£563

Folio 5   *Motor Van Account*

| Jan. 15 | Bank | CB1 | £500 |

Folio 6   *Electricity Account*

| Jan. 31 | Bank | CB1 | £15 |

Folio 7   *Purchases Returns Account*

| | | | | Jan. 31 | Sundries | PRB1 | £10 |

Folio 8   *Sales Returns Account*

| Jan. 31 | Sundries | SRB1 | £5 |

Folio 9   *Discount Allowed Account*

| Jan. 31 | Sundries | CB1 | £2 |

Folio 10   *Discount Received Account*

| | | | | Jan. 31 | Sundries | CB1 | £12 |

SALES LEDGER

Dr.   **Cr.**

Folio 1   *B. Finch Account*

| Jan. 4 | Goods | SDB1 | £70 | Jan. 25 | Bank | CB1 | £70 |

Folio 2   *R. Gold Account*

Jan. 4	Goods	SDB1	£55	Jan. 9	Returns	SRB1	£5
				17	Bank and		
					Discount	CB1	50
			£55				£55

Folio 3   *P. Smart Account*

| Jan. 20 | Goods | SDB1 | £125 |

PURCHASES LEDGER

Dr.   **Cr.**

Folio 1   *R. Smith Account*

Jan. 6	Returns	PRB1	£10	Jan. 3	Goods	PDB1	£50
22	Bank	CB1	40				
			£50				£50

Folio 2   *D. Jones Account*

| Jan. 7 | Bank and | | | Jan. 3 | Goods | PDB1 | £250 |
| | Discount | CB1 | £250 | | | | |

Folio 3   *T. West Account*

| | | | | Jan. 29 | Goods | PDB1 | £63 |

Folio 1   PURCHASES DAY BOOK

Jan. 3	R. Smith	PL1	£50
	D. Jones	PL2	250
29	T. West	PL3	63
			£363
			Folio IL4

Folio 1   SALES DAY BOOK

Jan. 4	B. Finch	SL1	£70
	R. Gold	SL2	55
20	P. Smart	SL3	125
			——
			£250

Folio IL3

Folio 1   PURCHASES RETURNS BOOK

Jan. 6	R. Smith	PL1	£10

Folio IL7

Folio 1   SALES RETURNS BOOK

Ján. 9	R. Gold	SL2	£5

Folio IL8

Trial Balance as at 31 January

		Dr.	Cr.
		£	£
CB1	Cash	170	
CB1	Bank	25	
IL1	Capital		1,000
2	Wages	50	
3	Sales		370
4	Purchases	563	
5	Motor Van	500	
6	Electricity	15	
7	Purchases Returns		10
8	Sales Returns	5	
9	Discount Allowed	2	
10	Discount Received		12
PL3	T. West		63
SL3	P. Smart	125	
		——	——
		£1,455	£1,455

Examination Questions

Question 1

From the following information calculate the capital of J. Scoles and prepare a Balance Sheet as at 31 March.

Assets at 31 Mar.—Motor Car £500, Plant £300, Stock £1,000, Debtors £700, and Cash £50.
Liabilities at 31 Mar.—Creditors £600 and Loan from Brown & Co. £100.

Question 2

Record the following transactions in the appropriate Day Books and post to the Ledger.

Jan. 2 Bought on credit from R. Grass:
        3 Filing Cabinets at £30 each
        2 Desks at £40 each.
    4 Bought on credit from W. Hirst:
        4 Chairs at £10 each
        2 Adding Machines at £65 each.
    6 Sold on credit to J. Bamford:
        1 Adding Machine at £90
        Less: 20% Trade Discount.
    7 Returned to R. Grass:
        1 Filing Cabinet damaged in transit £30.
  10 Sold on credit to R. Larch:
        1 Chair at £15
        1 Desk at £55.
  14 R. Larch returned the chair purchased by him on Jan. 10 as unsuitable.
  17 Sold to T. Holly:
        1 Desk at £80 *less* 10% Trade Discount.

Question 3

W. Branch has three departments in his business:

1. Toys
2. Books
3. Cigarettes and Tobacco.

You are required to rule a suitable Purchases Day Book and enter the following transactions:

Mar.	3 Purchased on credit from Tobacco Co.	
	10,000 cigarettes	£125
	5 Purchased on credit from Smith & Co.	
	40 Paperback Novels	15
	7 Purchased on credit from Smith & Jones	
	100 Jigsaw Puzzles	50
	10 Card Games	5
	12 Purchased on credit from Tobacco Co.	
	20,000 Cigarettes	260
	Carton of Tobacco	150
	16 Purchased on credit from Brown & Read	
	30 Paperback Novels	12
	20 Purchased on credit from Games & Co.	
	4 Conjuring Sets	6

Question 4

Using a two-column Cash Book record the following transactions and balance the Cash Book at 31 October. Ledger postings are not required.

Oct.	1	Capital introduced by W. Tree in cash	£300
	3	Lodged in Bank	200
	5	Paid for Purchases in cash	25
	7	Cash Sales paid into Bank	30
	12	Paid for Purchases by cheque	100
	15	Paid Sundry Expenses in cash	10
	18	Paid Wages by cheque	25
	20	Withdrew cheque for Office cash	20
	26	Cash Sales	50
	29	Paid Insurance by cheque	10
	31	Paid into Bank from office cash	80

Question 5

You are required to enter the following transactions in a three-column Cash Book and bring down the balances at 31 May:

May	1	P. Smyth commenced business with £1,000 in cash	
	3	Paid into Bank	£800
	5	Purchased Goods by cheque	£300
	7	Sold Goods for cash	£30
	9	Paid Wages in cash	£15
	12	Sent W. Brown cheque in settlement of his account of £100, *less* 5% discount	
	15	Cash Sales paid to bank	£150
	17	Received cheque from M. Williams	£175
		in full settlement of his account amounting to £180	
	19	Paid sundry expenses in cash	£5
	21	Sent H. Gill a cheque for £135 in settlement of his account	
	23	Received cheque for £120 from W. Spark	
	25	Paid Wages in cash	£20
	27	Sent cheque to J. Johnson in settlement of his account of £120, *less* $2\frac{1}{2}$% discount	
	31	Paid £110 into Bank from office cash	

Question 6

C. Coutts commenced business on 1 July with capital of £250 in cash. You are required to enter the transactions shown below in the appropriate books and then extract a Trial Balance.

July	2 Paid into Bank	£150
	3 Bought Goods by cash	30
	7 Purchased Goods on credit from J. White	300
	9 Paid Wages in cash	17
	12 Paid Sundry Expenses in cash	3
	15 Sold Goods on credit to M. Brown	60
	17 Paid J. White by cheque and was allowed 5% discount	
	19 Bought goods on credit from D. Bride	90
	21 M. Brown returned goods valued	5
	24 Paid rent by cheque	25
	27 Received cheque from M. Brown in settlement of his account.	
	28 Sold goods on credit to W. Crown	120
	Bought goods on credit from R. Rich	183
	29 Returned goods to D. Bride valued	8
	31 Received cheque from W. Crown *less* 5% discount	

Question 7

Enter the following transactions in the books of D. Waddell and thereafter extract a Trial Balance at 31 August.

Aug. 1 D. Waddell introduced capital of £500 and paid into the Bank
2 Withdrew from Bank £100 for office cash
3 Bought Goods on credit from T. Thornton £350
4 Paid for Motor Van by cheque £250
6 Sold Goods to R. Thomson on credit £200 *less* trade discount 20%
8 Paid Wages in cash £15
10 Cash Sales £70
12 Bought Goods on credit £700 from W. Greig
15 Received cheque *less* 5% discount from R. Thomson
16 Paid T. Thornton amount due to him *less* 2½% discount
18 Paid rent by cheque £30
20 Returned Goods to W. Greig £50
21 Sold Goods to R. Smith on credit £80
23 Bought Goods on credit from J. Flynn £100
25 R. Smith returned damaged goods £5
28 Paid for Shop Fittings by cheque £95
31 Paid Sundry Expenses in cash £10
Paid into Bank from office cash £50

2 Preparation of Trading and Profit and Loss Accounts and Balance Sheets

2.1 INTRODUCTION

So far only the recording of the basic entries in the books of original entry and ledgers have been discussed and it has been seen that a Trial Balance can be extracted at any point in time to prove the arithmetical accuracy of the postings. The accounting process does not cease on the extraction of a trial balance since the prime reason for recording entries in business books is to facilitate the preparation of Trading and Profit and Loss Accounts to establish whether a profit or loss has been made during the period under review and also a Balance Sheet to ascertain the assets and liabilities of the business at the end of the accounting period. To prepare these statements it is necessary to close off the revenue income and expenditure accounts to the Trading and Profit and Loss Accounts and to list the remaining balances in the Balance Sheet differentiating between assets and liabilities.

2.2 TRADING ACCOUNT AND PROFIT AND LOSS ACCOUNTS

2.21 TRADING ACCOUNT

The Trading Account is a ledger account and is prepared to calculate the 'gross' or 'trading' profit for a period. In this section of the final accounts it is usual to find the following items:

On the Debit side	On the Credit side
Stock at beginning of period	Sales (*less* sales returns)
Purchases (*less* purchases returns)	Stock at end of period
Carriage Inwards	
Wages (if not shown in Profit and Loss Account)	

The difference between the two sides, provided the credit side is in excess of the debit, will be the gross profit for the period which is then transferred to the credit side of the Profit and Loss Account. If a gross loss is made the entries are reversed.

2.22   ACCOUNTING ENTRIES TO TRANSFER BALANCES TO TRADING ACCOUNT

The balances appearing in the accounts referred to in the previous section are transferred to the Trading Account by means of journal entry shown in the illustration below.

Question

The balance shown in the Purchases Account at 31 December is £1,000. Show the Purchases Account and the Trading Account after the transfer is completed together with the relevant journal entry.

Suggested Solution:

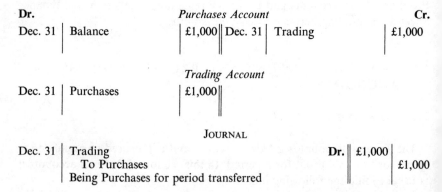

Dr.		*Purchases Account*				Cr.
Dec. 31	Balance	£1,000	Dec. 31	Trading		£1,000

Trading Account

Dec. 31	Purchases	£1,000

JOURNAL

Dec. 31	Trading		Dr.	£1,000	
	To Purchases				£1,000
	Being Purchases for period transferred				

All other amounts affecting the Trading Account are transferred in a similar fashion. It should be noted that entries recorded therein must follow the double entry principle. In solutions to questions requiring a Trading Account it is customary to omit the dates from both debit and credit sides but include the period covered by the Trading Account in the heading at the top of the account.

e.g. Trading Account for year ended 31 December.

2.23   TREATMENT OF STOCK

The treatment of the opening and closing amounts for stock in the Stock Account presents some difficulty to students. An example given below illustrates the entries in the Stock Account.

Question

At the beginning of Year 2 the stock amounted to £1,000 and appeared as a debit balance in the Stock Account. At the end of Year 2 the stock was valued at £1,500. Show the Stock Account recording these amounts and the appropriate transfers to Trading Account at the end of Year 2.

Suggested Solution:

Dr.			*Stock Account*		Cr.
Year 2	Balance	£1,000	Year 2 Trading		£1,000[1]
Year 2	Trading	£1,500[2]	Year 2 Balance		£1,500
Year 3	Balance	£1,500[3]			

Notes: 1. The balance of the opening stock is transferred to the Trading Account at the end of Year 2. In Journal form:

Dr. Trading
Cr. Stock

2. The value of the closing stock is debited to the Stock and credited to the Trading Account at the end of Year 2.

3. The balance of the closing stock is brought down to the beginning of the new period.

2.24   PROFIT AND LOSS ACCOUNT

The purpose of preparing a Profit and Loss Account is to determine the profit or loss for a period of trading. Profit is the surplus after charging all revenue expenses of the business against gross profit and other revenue income. A loss arises if the position is reversed.

The amounts of expenses and income are transferred to the Profit and Loss Account in much the same way as the items from the ledger to the Trading

Account. The Profit and Loss Account, like the Trading Account, is a ledger account and consequently all amounts posted to it must observe the double entry principle and also be shown in journal form.

2.25   ACCOUNTING ENTRIES REQUIRED TO TRANSFER BALANCE TO PROFIT AND LOSS ACCOUNT

The balance appearing in the Electricity Account at 31 December amounts to £200. Show the Electricity Account and the Profit and Loss Account after the transfer is completed together with the required journal entry.

Solution:

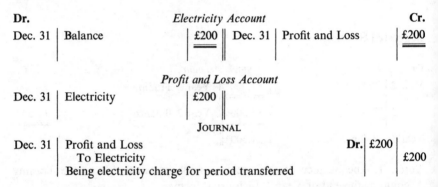

Dr.		*Electricity Account*				Cr.
Dec. 31	Balance	£200	Dec. 31	Profit and Loss		£200

Profit and Loss Account

Dec. 31	Electricity	£200	

JOURNAL

Dec. 31	Profit and Loss	Dr.	£200	
	To Electricity			£200
	Being electricity charge for period transferred			

The Profit and Loss Account is usually headed: Profit and Loss Account for Year ended 31 December—thus eliminating the need for recording dates on both debit and credit sides of the account.

All other items of revenue expenditure are transferred in a similar way. The entry for revenue income is, of course, reversed. The remaining balance on the Profit and Loss Account after all postings have been completed will be transferred, by journal entry, to the proprietor's Capital Account thus closing the Profit and Loss Account.

2.3   TREATMENT OF BALANCES ON ASSET AND LIABILITY ACCOUNTS

After the revenue expenditure and income have been transferred to either the Trading or Profit and Loss Accounts there will be accounts remaining in the ledger on which balances still appear. These accounts will represent assets and liabilities (including Capital Account) and will be shown as such in the

Balance Sheet. It must be observed that these accounts are not closed off to the Balance Sheet since this financial statement is not a ledger account but a list of assets and liabilities as at a particular point in time. After the completion of the Balance Sheet the balances remaining on these accounts will be brought down to the new period.

Example

Dr.		*Motor Car Account*			Cr.
Year 2	Balance	£5,000	Year 2	Balance	£6,000
	Bank	1,000			
		£6,000			£6,000
Year 3	Balance	£6,000			

The balance on the above account at the end of Year 2 will be shown as £6,000 on the Balance Sheet drawn up at that date.

Question

Using the balances recorded in the Trial Balance in the solution to Question 1.9 in Chapter 1, you are required to open the relevant ledger accounts to record the balances at 31 January and thereafter to close them off to the Trading and Profit and Loss Accounts. A Balance Sheet has also to be prepared as at 31 January. Stock at 31 January amounts to £300. Wages are to be shown in the Profit and Loss Account.

Trial Balance as at 31 January

		Dr.	Cr.
CB1	Cash	£170	
CB1	Bank	25	
IL1	Capital		£1,000
2	Wages	50	
3	Sales		370
4	Purchases	563	
5	Motor Van	500	
6	Electricity	15	
7	Purchases Returns		10
8	Sales Returns	5	
9	Discount Allowed	2	
10	Discount Received		12
PL3	T. West		63
SL3	P. Smart	125	
		£1,455	£1,455

IMPERSONAL LEDGER

Dr.	*Folio 1*		Capital Account			Cr.
Jan. 31	Balance c/d	£1,057	Jan. 31	Balance	£1,000
			Jan. 31	Profit and Loss	57
		£1,057			£1,057
			Feb. 1	Balance b/d	£1,057

	Folio 2		Wages Account			
Jan. 31	Balance	£50	Jan. 31	Profit and Loss	£50

	Folio 3		Sales Account			
Jan. 31	Sales Returns	£5	Jan. 31	Balance	£370
	Trading	365			
		£370			£370

	Folio 4		Purchases Account			
Jan. 31	Balance	£563	Jan. 31	Purchases Returns	£10
			Jan. 31	Trading	553
		£563			£563

	Folio 5		Motor Van Account			
Jan. 31	Balance	£500	Jan. 31	Balance c/d	£500
Feb. 1	Balance b/d	£500			

	Folio 6		Electricity Account			
Jan. 31	Balance	£15	Jan. 31	Profit and Loss	£15

	Folio 7		Purchases Returns Account			
Jan. 31	Purchases	£10	Jan. 31	Balance	£10

	Folio 8		Sales Returns Account			
Jan. 31	Balance	£5	Jan. 31	Sales	£5

Dr. *Folio 9*   *Discount Allowed Account*   **Cr.**

| Jan. 31 | Balance | £2 | Jan. 31 | Profit and Loss | £2 |

Folio 10   *Discount Received Account*

| Jan. 31 | Profit and Loss | £12 | Jan. 31 | Balance | £12 |

Folio 11   *Stock Account*

| Jan. 31 | Trading | £300 | Jan. 31 | Balance c/d | £300 |
| Feb. 1 | Balance b/d | £300 | | | |

SALES LEDGER

Folio 3   *P. Smart Account*

| Jan. 31 | Balance | £125 | Jan. 31 | Balance c/d | £125 |
| Feb. 1 | Balance b/d | £125 | | | |

PURCHASES LEDGER

Folio 3   *T. West Account*

| Jan. 31 | Balance c/d | £63 | Jan. 31 | Balance | £63 |
| | | | Feb. 1 | Balance b/d | £63 |

JOURNAL

Jan. 31	Purchases Returns	**Dr.**	£10	
	To Purchases			£10
	Being transfer of Purchases Returns for period			
	Sales	**Dr.**	5	
	To Sales Returns			5
	Being transfer of Sales Returns for period			
	Trading	**Dr.**	553	
	To Purchases			553
	Being Purchases for period transferred			
	Sales	**Dr.**	365	
	To Trading			365
	Being Sales for period transferred			
	Stock	**Dr.**	300	
	To Trading			300
	Being valuation of stock in hand at end of period			

JOURNAL—*(contd.)*

Profit and Loss **Dr.**	67		
To Wages			50
Electricity			15
Discount Allowed			2
Being Expenses for period transferred			
Discount Received **Dr.**	12		
To Profit and Loss			12
Being Income for period transferred			
Profit and Loss **Dr.**	57		
To Capital			57
Being Profit for period transferred			

CASH BOOK

Dr.   *Folio 1*   **Cr.**

		Cash	Bank			Cash	Bank
Jan. 31	Balances	£170	£25	Jan. 31	Balances c/d	£170	£25
Feb. 1	Balances b/d	£170	£25				

C. BROWN

Trading Account for Month ended 31 January

Purchases	£553	Sales	£365
Gross Profit carried down	112	Stock at end	300
	£665		£665

Profit and Loss Account for Month ended 31 January

Wages	£50	Gross Profit brought down	£112
Electricity	15	Discount Received	12
Discount Allowed	2		
Profit for month transferred to			
Capital Account	57		
	£124		£124

Balance Sheet as at 31 January

Capital Account			*Assets*	
Capital Introduced at			Motor Van	£500
1 Jan.	£1,000		Stock	300
Add: Profit for Month	57		Debtor	125
	——	1,057	Bank	25
			Cash	170
Liabilities				
Creditor		63		
		£1,120		£1,120

Notes: 1. The Stock at end has been shown on the credit side of the Trading Account in this problem but it is more often recorded as a deduction from Purchases on the debit side as illustrated later in the book.

2. The Assets in the Balance Sheet are usually grouped under Fixed Assets and Current Assets as will be seen in later examples.

2.4 ACCRUED AND PREPAID CHARGES

To make an accurate calculation of profit or loss for a particular trading period it is necessary to examine carefully the expenses of the business to determine those which have been incurred but not paid at the end of the trading period and also those which have been paid prior to the expiration of the period to which they relate.

These amounts are then listed and adjusted by means of journal entry in the relevant ledger accounts after all the postings from the books of original entry have been recorded in the ledger but prior to closing off the ledger accounts. The nominal accounts which are commonly subject to this type of adjustment are wages, rent, rates, insurance, telephone, and heating and lighting. Other accounts may require to be adjusted in this way to ensure that the correct charge for the trading period is transferred to the Profit and Loss Account. The accounting terms used to denote these adjustments are Accrued Charges and Prepaid or Unexpired Charges.

2.41 ACCRUED CHARGES

Expenses which have been incurred for the period but have not been paid or recorded are known as accrued expenses or charges. It is necessary to adjust the relevant ledger accounts for those expenses so that the existing charge in the account is increased by the amount of the accrual, and the liability is then recorded. For example, if wages are paid on each Friday and the accounting period ends on some other day then an entry will require to be made to adjust for the unpaid and unrecorded wages. This adjustment is made by journal entry in the first instance.

Wages (Old Period)   **Dr.**
  To Wages (New Period)
Being wages due and unpaid at end of
  accounting period.

It is better to make the adjustment for the accrual in the Wages Account rather than open a Suspense Account to record the accrued element.

Question

The Rent Account in the books of AB & Co., appears as follows:

Dr.		*Rent Account*			Cr.
Mar. 31	Bank	£120			
June 30	Bank	120			
Sept. 30	Bank	120			

Rent of £120 per quarter is paid in arrear on 31 March, 30 June, 30 September, and 31 December. Annual accounts are made up to 31 December. You are required to show the Rent Account after making any adjustments necessary at the year end and also to show the amount which will appear for rent in the Profit and Loss Account and Balance Sheet at 31 December.

Suggested Solution:

Since the rent due for the three months ended 31 December, amounting to £120, has not been included in the Rent Account it will require to be debited to the account before any transfer to the Profit and Loss Account is made.
In journal form the entry is:

> Dec. 31   Rent (Old Period)   **Dr.**   £120
> To Rent (New Period)   £120
> Being three months rent accrued at date.

Dr.		*Rent Account*			Cr.
Mar. 31	Bank	£120	Dec. 31	Profit and Loss	£480
June 30	Bank	120			
Sept. 30	Bank	120			
Dec. 31	Balance (accrual)	120			
		£480			£480
			Jan. 1	Balance (accrual)	£120

Profit and Loss Account (Extract from Debit side)
Rent   £480

Note: It is not necessary to show the accrued amount separately in the Profit and Loss Account.

Balance Sheet (Extract from Liabilities side)
Current Liabilities
Accrued Charge   £120

Note: It is not usual in the Balance Sheet of trading concerns to detail the accrued charges. A separate list of the individual amounts is prepared and the total transferred to the Balance Sheet under the narrative 'accrued charges'.

2.42 PREPAID CHARGES

Prepaid charges or expenses are amounts which have been paid before the expiration of the period to which they relate. To deal with this accounting problem the Expense Account is reduced by the unexpired amount and the latter sum treated as an asset in the Balance Sheet. For example if an annual insurance premium is paid on 1 April and the firm's financial year ends on 31 December then the Insurance Account will require to be credited with three months' premium to ensure that a correct charge for insurance is transferred to the Profit and Loss Account. This unexpired amount will be shown as a current asset in the Balance Sheet at 31 December. The adjustment is made by journal entry thus:

> Insurance (New Period)   **Dr.**
>   To Insurance (Old Period)
> Being amount of insurance premium unexpired at date.

Question

The Insurance Account in the books of AB & Co. appears as follows:

Dr.   *Insurance Account*   **Cr.**
June 30 | Bank | £300 |

The payment made on 30 June is in respect of an insurance premium covering the period of one year. AB & Co. make up their annual accounts to 31 December.

You are required to show the Insurance Account after making any adjustments necessary at the year end and also to show the amount which would appear for Insurance in the Profit and Loss Account and Balance Sheet at 31 December.

Suggested Solution:

As the insurance premium covers the period of a year the charge to be shown in the Profit and Loss Account to 31 December will only be from

30 June to 31 December. The balance of the charge, viz. £150, will be the unexpired or prepaid amount which will be carried forward to the succeeding period.

In journal form the entry is:

Dec. 31 Insurance (New Period)   **Dr.**   £150
          To Insurance (Old Period)   £150
Being six months' insurance premium unexpired at date.

Dr.			*Insurance Account*			**Cr.**
June 30	Bank	£300	Dec. 31	Balance (Prepaid)	£150	
				Profit and Loss	150	
		———			———	
		£300			£300	
Jan. 1	Balance (Prepaid)	£150				

Profit and Loss Account
(*Extract from Debit side*)
Insurance   £150

Note: Again it is not necessary to show separately the unexpired amount as a deduction in the Profit and Loss Account.

Balance Sheet
(*Extract from Assets side*)
Current Assets
                    Prepaid Charge   £150

Note: In the same way as accrued charges it is not usual to detail prepaid charges in the Balance Sheet. It is better to prepare a separate schedule listing the prepayments and only transferring the total to the Balance Sheet.

2.5   ACCRUED AND PREPAID INCOME

An adjustment is required when income has been earned but since it is not due and has not been received no record of the earning has been made before the end of the financial period. The adjustment for the accrued income (say interest) is

Interest (New Period)   **Dr.**
          To Interest (Old Period)
Being Interest earned to date but not received.

Conversely income may be received before it is earned. The amount of income which has been received but unearned is known as prepaid income. The adjusting entry is:

Interest (Old Period)   **Dr.**
   To Interest (New Period)
Being Interest received but unearned at date.

2.6 BAD DEBTS

Businesses to a large extent operate on credit. Credit is extended to customers with the intention that payment will be made within a defined period. Although care is taken in selecting the customers to whom credit terms may be granted, it is not always possible to collect all the amounts due within the stipulated time limit and in some cases payment may not be received at all due to the insolvency of the debtor. If the debtor is unable to pay the balance owing, this amount is treated as a bad debt and written off to the Profit and Loss Account as a business expense.

Question

T. Smith has been owing R. White £20 since 1 January and is now unable to make payment of this amount due to his insolvency. White decides to write the balance off as a bad debt at the end of his financial year which is 31 December. You are required to show T. Smith's Account and the Bad Debts Account as they would appear in White's Books and also the charge shown in the Profit and Loss Account for Bad Debts at 31 December.

Suggested Solution:

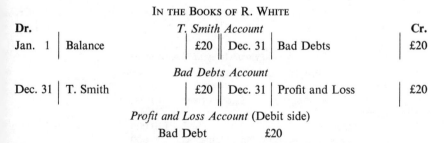

IN THE BOOKS OF R. WHITE

Dr.			*T. Smith Account*			Cr.
Jan. 1	Balance	£20	Dec. 31	Bad Debts		£20

Bad Debts Account

Dec. 31	T. Smith	£20	Dec. 31	Profit and Loss	£20

Profit and Loss Account (Debit side)

Bad Debt   £20

Note: The transfer of the balance of T. Smith's Account to Bad Debts Account and the resulting balance on the latter account to Profit and Loss Account are made by journal entry.

2.61   PROVISION FOR BAD AND DOUBTFUL DEBTS

At the end of each financial period it is only prudent to examine all debtors' balances in the sales ledger to establish not only those amounts which are irrecoverable but also to determine any accounts which are overdue and unlikely to be paid. An amount should be set aside as a provision for those amounts which are unlikely to be settled. In some businesses a fixed percentage of debtors' balances is made each year as a provision for bad debts. Irrespective of the method used the purpose is to create a provision for bad debts which when deducted from the total debtors' balances leaves the amount expected to be ultimately collected.

Question

The total debtors at 31 December in the books of J. Thomson amounts to £10,000. A provision for bad debts amounting to 5% of total debtors is to be created.

You are required to write up the Provision for Bad Debts Account and show the relevant entries in the Profit and Loss Account and Balance Sheet at 31 December. Journal entries where necessary are required to be shown.

Suggested Solution:

IN THE BOOKS OF J. THOMSON

JOURNAL

Dec. 31	Profit and Loss Dr.	£500	
	To Provision for Bad Debts		£500
	Being provision of 5% of debtors created this date		

LEDGER

Dr.   *Provision for Bad Debts Account*   **Cr.**

| | | | Dec. 31 | Profit and Loss | £500 |

Profit and Loss Account (Debit side)

Provision for Bad Debts   £500

Balance Sheet (Extract from Assets side)

Current Assets
Debtors	£10,000	
Less: Provision for Bad Debts	500	
	——— £9,500	

Note: When a provision for bad debts is created no entries are made in the debtors' accounts in the sales ledger. The balance on the Provision for Bad

Debts Account is deducted from the total debtors in the Balance Sheet but remains in the nominal ledger as a credit balance to be carried down to the succeeding year.

Question

In the books of W. Scarlet on 1 January there was a balance on the Provision for Bad Debts Account of £500. At the end of the year it was decided to write off J. Smith's account of £250 as a bad debt and to create a provision for bad debts of £600. The total debtors at 31 December before writing off the bad debts amounted to £12,000. You are required to write up the necessary journal entries and ledger accounts to record the above together with the entries as they would appear in the Profit and Loss Account and Balance Sheet at 31 December.

Suggested Solution:

IN THE BOOKS OF W. SCARLET

JOURNAL

Dec. 31	Provision for Bad Debts	**Dr.**	£250	
	To J. Smith			£250
	Being the balance on J. Smith's account written off as bad			
	Profit and Loss	**Dr.**	£350	
	To Provision for Bad Debts			£350
	Being amount required to increase provision to £600			

LEDGER

Dr.   *J. Smith Account*   **Cr.**

Jan. 1	Balance	£250	Dec. 31	Bad Debts Provision	£250

Bad Debts Provision Account

Dec. 31	J. Smith	£250	Jan. 1	Balance	£500
	Balance	600	Dec. 31	Profit and Loss	350
		£850			£850
			Jan. 1	Balance	£600

Note: If a Provision for Bad Debts Account is opened any amount written off as bad is usually transferred to this account and not to Bad Debts Account.

Profit and Loss Account (Debit side)

Provision for Bad Debts   £350

Balance Sheet (Extract from Assets side)

Current Assets

	Debtors	£11,750	
	Less: Provision for Bad Debts	600	
			£11,150

Note: If an amount is written off as bad it is deducted from the total debtors before the latter amount is recorded in the Balance Sheet. The new provision for bad debts is deducted from the debtors in the usual way.

2.62 BAD DEBTS RECOVERED

Occasionally a debt which has previously been written off as bad will be paid in full or part at a later date. This type of transaction is recorded in the following manner:

Dr. Bank with the amount of the recovery
Cr. Debtor's Account
Dr. Debtor's Account
Cr. Bad Debts Recovered.

The balance on the Bad Debts Recovered Account is transferred to the Profit and Loss Account at the end of the financial year.

2.7 PROVISION FOR DISCOUNT ALLOWED

If customers are allowed cash discount for prompt payment then theoretically an estimate of the probable discount to be allowed should be made and an adjustment recorded in the firm's books at the end of each financial period. The amount of this provision will be debited to the Discount Allowed Account before the balance is transferred to Profit and Loss Account and it will be deducted from the total debtors in the Balance Sheet so that the balance shown is that which is due to be collected.

Question

In the books of R. Townsend at 31 December the debtors were £12,000 and the provision for bad debts £600. It is decided to create a provision for discount allowed at the rate of $2\frac{1}{2}\%$ on debtors.

You are required to prepare the journal entry to record this adjustment and to show how the debtors will appear in the Balance Sheet at 31 December.

Suggested Solution:

IN THE BOOKS OF R. TOWNSEND

JOURNAL

Dec. 31	Profit and Loss **Dr.**	£285	
	To Provision for Discount Allowed		£285
	Being amount of discount provision at 2½% of £11,400		

Note: The provision for discount allowed is calculated on the total debtors less the provision for bad debts, viz. £12,000 − £600 = £11,400.

Balance Sheet (Extract from Assets side)

Current Assets

Debtors		£12,000	
Less: Provision for Bad Debts	£600		
Provision for Discount Allowed	285	885	
			£11,115

2.8 PROVISION FOR DISCOUNT RECEIVED

As well as creating a provision for discount allowed on customers' balances many businesses also create a provision for discount to be received on amounts due to creditors. The accounting technique used to record this adjustment is similar to the previous example. The Discount Received Account is increased by the amount of the provision and it is then shown as a deduction from creditors in the Balance Sheet at the end of the trading period.

Question

In the books of R. Townsend at 31 December the creditors were £10,000. A provision for discount receivable is to be created at the rate of 5%. The balance on the Discount Received Account before adjusting for this provision is £2,000.

You are required to write up the Discount Received Account at 31 December and bring down the balance on that account to the succeeding period.

Suggested Solution:

IN THE BOOKS OF R. TOWNSEND

LEDGER

Dr.		*Discount Received Account*			Cr.
Dec. 31	Profit and Loss	£2,500	Dec. 31	Total Discount from Cash Book	£2,000
				Balance (discounts receivable from creditors per Journal)	£500
		£2,500			£2,500
Jan. 1	Balance	£500			

2.9 CLASSIFICATION OF ACCOUNTS IN THE PROFIT AND LOSS ACCOUNT

The Profit and Loss Account forms an integral part of the accounting system since it is a summary of all the nominal accounts, i.e. profits and losses or income and expenditure resulting in the determination of the profit or loss for the period. Although the items shown in this account are broadly classified as revenue expenditure and income, it is useful for the purpose of analysing and interpreting the results brought out in this account that they should be classified under the following headings:

ADMINISTRATION

SELLING

FINANCE

Using these headings a Profit and Loss Account may be drafted thus:

Profit and Loss Account for Year ended 31 December

Administration

Office Salaries			Gross Profit brought down	
Rent, Rates, and Insurance			Interest: Bank Investments	
Heating and Lighting			Discount Received	
Printing and Stationery			Miscellaneous	
Audit Fees			(Detail as required)	
Legal Expenses				
Telephone and Postage				
Depreciation				
(Office Assets)				
General Office Expenses				
		———		
Selling				
Salesmen's Salaries and				
Commission				
Travelling Expenses				
Carriage Outwards				
		———		
Finance				
*Discount Allowed				
Bank Overdraft				
Interest				
*Bad Debts				
		———		
Profit for Year				
		———		———
	£			£
	═══			═══

* These items could be treated as Selling Expenses.

Note that no classification of revenue income has been made on the credit side of the Profit and Loss Account.

The question following is a typical examination problem where Trading and Profit and Loss Accounts and a Balance Sheet have to be prepared from a Trial Balance with adjustments.

Question

You are required to prepare a Trading and Profit and Loss Account for the year ended 31 December and a Balance Sheet as at that date from the undernoted Trial Balance taken from the books of R. James.

Trial Balance as at 31 December

	Dr.	Cr.
Cash at Bank	£540	
Fixtures and Fittings	1,020	
Purchases and Sales Returns	190	£125
Travelling Expenses	110	
Rent and Rates	170	
Purchases	18,120	
Buildings	6,000	
Debtors and Creditors	5,350	4,160
Delivery Vehicles	2,425	
Cash on hand	75	
Salaries of Salesmen	5,120	
Stock 1 Jan.	6,110	
Sales		33,110
Discounts	535	570
Lighting and Heating	280	
Bad Debt Provision 1 Jan.		290
Delivery Vehicle Expenses	1,000	
Insurance	210	
Capital Account		12,000
Drawings	2,000	
Office Salaries	1,000	
	£50,255	£50,255

The following additional information is given:

1. Stock on hand at 31 December £2,140.
2. The following items have to be accrued:

    Salaries of Salesmen £135
    Travelling Expenses   £10

3. Insurance has to be prepaid £15.
4. Bad Debts to be written off as irrecoverable £60. The provision for bad debts to be adjusted to 5% of debtors.
5. Make provision for discount allowed to customers at $2\frac{1}{2}\%$ of debtors. Calculations to nearest £.

Suggested Solution:

R. JAMES

Trading Account for Year ended 31 December

Purchases (*less* returns)	£17,995	Sales (*less* returns)	£32,920
Add: Stock 1 Jan.	6,110		
	24,105		
Less: Stock 31 Dec.	2,140		
Cost of Goods Sold	21,965		
Gross Profit	10,955		
	£32,920		£32,920

Profit and Loss Account for Year ended 31 December

Administration			Gross Profit	£10,955
Office Salaries	£1,000		Discount Received	570
Insurance	195			
Lighting and Heating	280			
Rent and Rates	170			
		1,645		
Selling				
Salaries of Salesmen	5,255			
Delivery Vehicle Expenses	1,000			
Travelling Expenses	120			
		6,375		
Finance				
Discount Allowed	661			
Provision for Bad Debts	34			
		695		
Profit for Year		2,810		
		£11,525		£11,525

Balance Sheet as at 31 December

Capital			Fixed Assets			
As at 1 Jan.	£12,000		Buildings			£6,000
Add: Profit for			Fixtures and			
Year	2,810		Fittings			1,020
			Delivery			
			Vehicles			2,425
	14,810					9,445
Less: Drawings	2,000					
		£12,810				
Current Liabilities			Current Assets			
			Stock		2,140	
Creditors	4,160		Debtors	5,290		
Accrued Charges	145		*Less:* Provision			
		4,305	for Bad Debts	£264		
			Provision			
			for Dis-			
			count	126	390	
					4,900	
			Prepaid Charge		15	
			Cash at Bank		540	
			Cash on Hand		75	
						7,670
		£17,115				£17,115

Working Notes:

1. Calculation of Discount Allowed:

Per Trial Balance	£535
Add: Provision of $2\frac{1}{2}\%$ on Debtors	
$[5,350 - (60 + 264)]$	126
	£661

2. Calculation of Provision for Bad Debts:

Bad Debts written off	£60
Add: New Provision 5% $(5,350-60)$	264
	324
Less: Old Provision	290
Per Profit and Loss Account	£34

Examination Questions

Question 1

The following is the Trial Balance of A. Wood on 31 December:

	Dr.	Cr.
Capital Account 1 Jan.		£1,750
Salaries	£1,770	
Debtors and Creditors	1,820	490
Discounts	290	130
Purchases and Sales	3,110	6,570
Rent and Rates	320	
Drawings	850	
Bank		810
Cash	60	
Stock 1 Jan.	840	
Office Equipment	360	
Repairs and Renewals	220	
Sundry Expenses	110	
	£9,750	£9,750

You are required to open Accounts and enter the above balances and prepare Trading and Profit and Loss Accounts for year ended 31 December and a Balance Sheet as at that date. Stock at 31 December was valued at £900. The closing entries must be shown and balances brought down in the relevant accounts at 31 December.

Question 2

The following amounts are shown in the Trial Balance extracted from the books of A. Smith on 31 December:

	Dr.	Cr.
Wages	£1,000	
Loan Interest	500	
Rates	100	
Advertising	200	
Interest on Dividends		50
Rent Received		70

Adjustments have to be made as follows:

Wages due and unpaid	£50
Loan interest unpaid	30
Rates paid in advance	20
Advertising cost to be carried forward	150
Interest on Dividends due to be received	20
Rent received in advance	10

Show the Ledger Accounts recording the above.

Question 3

The Debtors in the Books of A. Reid amount to £2,000 at 31 December.
It is decided that a provision for Bad Debts of 5% of Debtors be created at
that date.

You are required to show the journal entries to create the provision and
give the relevant ledger accounts. Show also how the Debtors would appear
in A. Reid's Balance Sheet.

Question 4

It is decided that the provision for Bad Debts should remain at 5% of
Debtors. Debtors at 31 December amount to £9,000 and the existing provision
for Bad Debts is £500.

Show the entries required to maintain the provision at 5% of Debtors.

Question 5

You are given the following information about transactions involving the
debtors of Jack Jones Ltd., during the year ended 31 January Year 5:

(a) On 3 March Year 4, Smith Ltd. was liquidated when its account in the
books of Jack Jones Ltd. showed a balance of £330. On 5 March Year
4, a cheque for £150 which Jack Jones Ltd. had received from Smith
Ltd. on 1 March Year 4, was dishonoured. Smith Ltd. paid a first
dividend of £0·25 in the £ on 30 August Year 4. On 25 January Year 5
the Liquidator informed Jack Jones Ltd. that a final dividend of £0·1
in the £ would be paid in February Year 5, and provision should be
made for this in closing off the books at 31 January Year 5.

(b) In December Year 3, the company had written off a debt of £85 due by
J. Robertson & Son, which was deemed irrecoverable. On 2 May Year
4, J. Robertson & Son paid the company £80 in full settlement of the
debt.

(c) At 31 January Year 5, it was considered that the following debts were
doubtful and that a provision to the extent of 50% of each should be
made:

A. Anderson	£50
B. Benson	£120
C. Cadzow	£44

You are required to show by means of journal entries, with full narrations
how the above information should be incorporated in the books of Jack
Jones Ltd. Ignore Debtors Control Account.   (C.A. Adapted

Question 6

P. Waters is a Merchant and the following amounts were extracted from his books on 31 December:

Stock 1 Jan.	£6,012	
Bank	1,891	
Property	2,500	
Capital		£8,937
Sundry Expenses	63	
Purchases	34,242	
Cash in Hand	176	
Telephone	17	
Rates	50	
Salaries	1,419	
Electricity	46	
Motor Vehicles	464	
Sales		36,749
Fixtures and Fittings	552	
Discount Allowed	69	
Returns	28	196
Bad Debts	13	
Insurance	96	
Creditors		4,203
Debtors	2,447	
	£50,085	£50,085

In preparing the Trading and Profit and Loss Accounts for the year ended 31 December and the Balance Sheet as at that date, the following additional information has to be taken into consideration:

(a) Stock at 31 December is valued at £5,012.
(b) Staff Salaries of £100 have to be accrued.
(c) Insurance has to be prepaid to the extent of £10.
(d) A new provision for Bad Debts to be created amounting to £160.
(e) A provision for discount allowed is to be made at the rate of $2\frac{1}{2}\%$ of debtors. (Workings to nearest £.)

Question 7

A. Munro is a Retailer and his Trial Balance at 31 December Year 5, was as follows:

Capital		£16,760
Debtors	£4,800	
Van Running Costs	208	
Sales		34,107
Motor Vans	1,500	
Discount Received		603
Discount Allowed	239	
Office Salaries	1,000	
Cash at Bank and on Hand	1,479	
Rates	419	
Purchases	29,338	
Drawings	1,250	
Advertising	687	
Buildings	5,000	
Salesmen's Wages	2,631	
Bad Debts	38	
Bank Overdraft Interest	24	
Lighting and Heating	495	
Furniture and Fittings	3,800	
Stock 1 Jan. Year 5	3,467	
Bad Debts Provision—1 Jan. Year 5		189
Creditors		4,716
	£56,375	£56,375

The following adjustments are to be made:

(a) Prepayments at 31 December Year 5:

Rates	£20
Van Insurance (included in van running costs)	£5

(b) Accruals at 31 December Year 5:

Salesmen's Wages	£125
Electricity	£10
Office Salaries	£15

(c) Advertising Expenditure to be carried forward amounts to £519.
(d) The Provision for Bad Debts is to be equal to 5% of Trade Debtors.
(e) Stock at 31 December Year 5 amounts to £3,500.
(f) Other Stocks at 31 December Year 5:

Coal for Heating	£11

(g) During June a fire at the firm's premises destroyed stock which had cost £1,000. The firm's Insurers have agreed to meet an insurance claim for the full amount. No entries have been made in the books in respect of the claim. The Stock in Trade at 31 December Year 5 shown above represents the stock actually held at that date.

(h) Make a provision for Discount Allowed of $2\frac{1}{2}\%$ of Debtors.

You are required to prepare a Trading and Profit and Loss Account for year ended 31 December Year 5, and a Balance Sheet at that date.

3 Bank Reconciliation Statement; Petty Cash Book; Correction of Errors

3.1 BANK RECONCILIATION STATEMENT

3.11 PURPOSE OF PREPARING THIS STATEMENT

The purpose of preparing a bank reconciliation statement is to agree the balance shown in the bank column of the cash book with that indicated on the bank statement. The preparation of this statement is usually the responsibility of the cashier. The normal practice adopted by most businesses is to maintain separate bank columns in the cash book. On the credit side are recorded cheques drawn and paid to creditors, etc. and on the debit side remittances from debtors lodged in the bank account. Similar information is recorded in the firm's account with the bank and a copy of this account is sent by the bank at regular intervals to the customer in the form of a bank statement. The balances in the cash book and the bank statement should agree but very rarely does this occur.

3.12 REASONS FOR BANK BALANCES NOT AGREEING

(a) A cheque may be debited in the cash book but not shown in the bank statement on the same day. This arises when a cheque is received and entered in the cash book but not lodged in the bank till a later date.

(b) A cheque drawn and credited in the cash book but not appearing in the bank statement on that date. This is a very common situation owing to the time lag from the date of drawing the cheque until the date it is presented to the bank for payment.

(c) Remittances credited in the bank statement but not recorded in the cash book until a later date. Occasionally the bank accepts payment direct from the customer's debtors or collects dividends from investments and credits these sums to the customer's account. The customer may not be notified of these transactions until he receives a bank statement.

(*d*) Payments appearing in the bank statement but not shown in the cash book until a later date. This occurs when the bank debits interest or bank charges to the customer's account and the customer is only notified of these amounts on receipt of the bank statement. The customer may also have arranged with the bank to pay certain items by banker's order but has omitted to record these in cash book on the appropriate date. In both cases the entries in the cash book will be delayed until the bank statement is received.

3.13 PROCEDURE IN PREPARING A BANK RECONCILIATION STATEMENT

A bank reconciliation statement is always drawn up as at a particular point in time and for that reason adjustments appear in the statement to deal with the matters mentioned in the previous section.

The procedure is firstly to adjust on the bank balance disclosed in the cash book any items which are entered in the bank statement but not in the bank columns of the cash book. The adjusted amount will represent the true bank balance in the cash book. Secondly, adjust on the bank statement balance the amount of any unpresented cheques and lodgments not yet credited by the bank. This adjusted bank statement balance should then agree with the bank balance in the cash book. The form of a bank reconciliation statement is shown below.

Bank Reconciliation Statement as at 31 December Year 2

Balance in bank per cash book		£520
Add: Amounts not entered in cash book but in		
bank statement		
Dividend on Investment	£10	
Payment made direct to bank by debtor	105	
	——	115
		635
Less: Amounts not entered in cash book but in		
bank statement		
Bank Charges	£3	
Bank Overdraft Interest	15	
	——	18
Adjusted Cash Book Balance		£617

Balance per Bank Statement		£502
Add: Cheques not yet credited—W. Smith	£110	
—H. Hay	45	
	——	155
		657
Less: Cheques drawn but not yet presented for payment—J. Thomson		40
Adjusted Bank Statement Balance		£617

Notes: 1. In the above presentation it has been assumed that there was a balance of cash at the Bank. If the position was altered and the bank account was overdrawn the adjustments shown above would be reversed.

2. Although the student has to have knowledge of the types of adjustments which may arise in this problem it is advisable not to use the above form of presentation exactly but to work through the adjustments in every solution. The reason for this is that many questions are worded differently and ask for a solution slightly different from the above.

The following question is solved using the foregoing draft form.

Question

On 31 December Year 9 John Smith's Cash Book showed a balance of £170 representing cash at bank. At that date the cashier checked the bank statement received from the bank with the cash book and all the amounts agreed with the exception of the following:

(*a*) The bank had paid an amount of £5 to a motoring organization. This amount had not been entered in the cash book.

(*b*) During the month of December the Bank had debited Smith's account with £10 in respect of bank charges. No record had been made in the cash book.

(*c*) John Smith's cashier had received a remittance from R. White for £100 on 31 December and entered the details in the cash book but this amount was not yet credited by the bank.

(*d*) The following cheques drawn and recorded in the cash book on 31 December had not yet been presented to the bank for payment:

T. Green	£50
W. Brown	£80

(*e*) The bank had credited to John Smith's account £20 in respect of share dividends but this had not been entered in the cash book.

You are required to draw up a bank reconciliation statement as at 31 December Year 9. The balance shown in the bank statement at that date was £205.

Suggested Solution:

Bank Reconciliation Statement as at 31 December Year 9

Balance in bank per cash book		£170
Add: Amount not entered in cash book but in bank statement		
Share Dividends		20
		£190
Less: Amounts not entered in cash book but in bank statement		
Payment to Motoring Organization	£5	
Bank Charges	10	
		15
Adjusted Cash Book Balance		£175
Balance per Bank Statement		£205
Add: Cheque not yet credited:		
R. White		100
		305
Less: Cheques drawn but not yet presented for payment:		
T. Green	£50	
W. Brown	80	
		130
Adjusted Bank Statement Balance		£175

3.2 PETTY CASH BOOK

3.21 PURPOSE OF KEEPING A PETTY CASH BOOK

Most businesses find it more convenient to record small cash transactions through a subsidiary book rather than enter them in the main cash book. This subsidiary book is known as the Petty Cash Book and is usually kept by a junior member of the accounting staff thus saving the main cashier's valuable time. The cash payments recorded in this way are small in value and generally repetitive in nature such as postages, travelling expenses, small items of stationery, cleaning materials, office tea, and other small items of office expenditure. Although the petty cash book is a subsidiary book it still forms part of the double entry accounting system of the business. It is linked with the principal cash book by the transfer made to it periodically, usually weekly or monthly, from the latter book.

3.22 METHODS USED TO RECORD ENTRIES IN PETTY CASH BOOK

Below are two methods in use for the writing up of petty cash books.

(a) *Where no Imprest Amount is given to the Petty Cashier*

Under this method the petty cashier is initially handed a sum of money by the main cashier to open up a petty cash book. When this takes place the petty cashier debits the petty cash book with the amount of the cash transfer and the main cashier credits the principal cash book with an equivalent sum. The petty cash book is principally a petty cash account in which receipts of cash are debited and cash payments credited. It differs slightly, however, from the conventional ledger account in so far as the credit side of the petty cash book is usually ruled in columnar form. The purpose of this layout is to enable similar items of expenditure to be grouped more easily. In this way a column is opened on the credit side of the petty cash book for each item of expenditure which is repetitive and a sundries column is kept for those expenses which occur at infrequent intervals. By preparing the petty cash book in analytical form the number of postings made from it to the impersonal ledger can be substantially reduced so saving a great deal of time and limiting the possibility of error. The petty cashier must obtain receipts for all expenditure paid from the petty cash book. When additional cash is required the petty cashier is reimbursed from the main cashier with a further sum of cash. By using this method the amount reimbursed by the cashier is not fixed and neither does it necessarily require to be equal to the expenditure previously incurred.

Accounting Entries in this Method are:

1. Dr. Petty Cash book with amount of cash transferred from principal cash book.
   Cr. Main Cash Book.
2. Dr. Petty Cash Book with any small items of cash income.
   Cr. Appropriate accounts in impersonal ledger, or sales ledger if received from a debtor.
3. Dr. Appropriate accounts in impersonal ledger with cash expenditure.
   Cr. Petty Cash Book.

Example of *Petty Cash Book* (Normal System of Balancing)

PETTY CASH BOOK

Receipts £	Folio	Date	Details	Voucher No.	Total £	Postages £	Stationery £	Travelling Expenses £	Cleaning £	Sundries £	Ledger Accounts £	Ledger Folio
30	CB25	Jan. 1	Cash									
		2	Postages	1	2	2						
		3	Bus Fares	2	1			1				
		5	Envelopes	3	2		2					
		7	Cleaning Materials	4	4				4			
		10	Postages	5	1	1						
		12	R. Brown	6	3						3	PL52
		16	Office Tea	7	1					1		
		19	Notepaper	8	2		2					
		23	Train Fare	9	5			5				
		27	Postages	10	1	1						
		31	Cleaning Materials	11	3				3			
					25	4	4	6	7	1	3	
						IL10	IL15	IL46	IL4	IL32		
			Balance		5							
£30					£30							
5		Feb. 1	Balance									

Notes: 1. The initial debit of £30 under cash book folio CB25 is the amount of cash transferred from the cash book for petty cash disbursements.

2. The folios appearing below the analysed columns are in respect of postings to the Impersonal Ledger.

3. The folio shown against the payment of £3 to R. Brown relates to the Purchases Ledger to which the payment would be posted.

4. In this method the petty cash book is balanced in a similar manner to any other ledger account and the balance carried down to the next period.

(*b*) *Where an Imprest Amount is given to the Cashier*

In this system, which is known as the 'Imprest' system, the main cashier allocates a fixed amount which should be sufficient to meet the petty cash expenditure for an agreed period of time. This fixed sum is often referred to as the cash 'float'. At the end of the agreed period, usually a week or a month, the sum expended by the petty cashier is refunded to him thus making the balance up to the original sum. This is the main difference from the previous method where the petty cashier received reimbursements from the cashier which did not necessarily equal the sum disbursed. Control over the petty cash balance is simpler under this system since at any time the cash in hand plus the amount expended from the last reimbursement should equal the cash 'float' or 'Imprest' amount.

Referring to the previous example the solution would have appeared as over if the petty cash book had been kept on the 'Imprest' system. No difference is made to the heading in the petty cash book in this system nor are the entries altered *with the exception of the balancing at the end of the period.*

PETTY CASH BOOK ('Imprest' System of Balancing)

Receipts	Folio	Date	Details	Voucher No.	Total	Postages	Stationery	Travelling Expenses	Cleaning	Sundries	Ledger Account	Ledger Folio
£					£	£	£	£	£	£	£	
30					25	4	4	6	7	1	3	
25	CB29	Jan. 31	Cash, Reimbursement									
			Balance		30							
£55					£55	IL10	IL15	IL46	IL4	IL32		
£30		Feb. 1	Balance									

Notes: 1. The postings to the ledger from the petty cash book are similar to the previous method.

2. In this system the cash reimbursement takes place prior to the balancing of the book and is equal to the amount of the cash expenditure for the period. The balance of cash in the petty cash book brought down after reimbursement must always equal the 'Imprest' amount.

3.3 CORRECTION OF ERRORS

3.31 INTRODUCTION

The fundamental principle of double entry accounting states that each transaction has a debit entry and a credit entry. By always observing this principle it is possible to extract a trial balance at the end of any accounting period and, if the accounts are correctly balanced, the total of the debit balances should be equal to the total of the credit balances. In other words it proves that debit and credit entries have been made for every transaction entered through the books. While this information is important an agreed trial balance does not necessarily indicate that every transaction which should have been recorded has been recorded, nor does it reveal that those transactions which have been recorded are recorded correctly. The types of errors which can occur although the trial balance is agreed are discussed in the next section.

3.32 TYPES OF ERRORS NOT REVEALED BY A TRIAL BALANCE

(a) *Error of Principle*

This type of error occurs where a transaction has been treated incorrectly by being posted to the wrong class of account. For example, Tom Black who is in business as a joiner purchases a motor van for use in his business. His bookkeeper posts this transaction to the debit of purchases account instead of motor vehicles account. This item has been charged incorrectly to a revenue account when it should have been posted to an asset account.

(b) *Error of Original Entry*

This happens where a transaction has been incorrectly recorded in a book of original entry and thereafter the incorrectly entered amount posted to the debit and credit sides of the ledger. For example, W. Smith makes a purchase of goods on credit for £120. The amount of the purchase is entered in the Purchases Day Book as £100 and this sum is posted to the creditor's account and the purchases account. Although the error has no effect on the trial balance, the purchases account and the creditor's account are both understated by £20.

(c) Error of Omission

This indicates that the whole transaction is not recorded in the books, i.e. no debit or credit entry is made. For example, a sales invoice for £100 was prepared in respect of goods sent to R. Green but was lost before it was recorded in the books. Again this would have no effect on the agreement of the trial balance.

(d) Error of Commission

If a transaction has been entered in an incorrect account although of the same class then this is known as an error of commission. For example, goods are purchased from D. Brown but the credit entry is posted in error to the account of C. Brown In this example the double entry has been completed and is arithmetically accurate but the wrong account was credited.

(e) Compensating Error

This arises where errors occur on one side of the ledger but are compensated by equalizing errors on the other side, e.g. the total of the Sales Day Book which amounted to £1,000 was posted to the credit of the Sales Account as £1,100 and the total of the Purchases Day Book which amounted to £700 was posted to the debit of the Purchases Account as £800. In this example the error of £100 in the posting to the Sales Account is compensated by the error of a similar sum to the Purchases Account without affecting the agreement of the Trial Balance.

3.33   SUSPENSE ACCOUNT

The trial balance does, however, reveal certain errors made in the recording of transactions. If the double entry for a transaction has not been completed arithmetically correctly then a difference will appear in the trial balance. If such a difference arises a Suspense Account is opened and the difference debited or credited to that account. The balance on the Suspense Account is entered in the trial balance so agreeing it. This is only a temporary expedient until such time as the difference is located when rectifying entries are made which will have the effect of eliminating the balance on the Suspense Account.

3.34   THE USE OF THE JOURNAL TO RECTIFY ERRORS

Where errors have been made in the recording of business transactions such entries should not be corrected by erasing them and substituting the correct entries in their place. The errors must be rectified by the use of the journal which is the orthodox and correct method of dealing with such matters. If members of the accounting staff are permitted to alter wrong entries by any other process then the business concerned is making it easier for staff, if they so desire, to perpetrate fraud.

The following question and solution illustrate the use of the journal as the method to rectify incorrect entries in business records.

Question

A Trial Balance, extracted from the books of Careless & Company at 30 September Year 2, did not balance and the difference of £304 was entered on the credit side of a Difference Suspense Account specially opened in the ledger. Draft Accounts were prepared from this Trial Balance and showed a net profit of £3,600, the Difference Suspense Account having been treated as a Sundry Creditor in the Balance Sheet.

Careless & Company do not maintain Control Accounts for Debtors or Creditors.

The following errors were subsequently discovered and the difference eliminated:

(a) The Bank Overdraft of £207 as shown in the Cash Book at 30 September Year 2 has been omitted from the Trial Balance.

(b) A payment of £54 to Baker, a trade creditor, had been correctly entered in the Cash Book but had been posted to the Personal Account as £45.

(c) The total Discount Received and Discount Allowed for the year amounting respectively to £86 and £45 had been posted from the Cash Book to the wrong sides of the Discount Account.

(d) A sales invoice for £148 dated 25 September Year 2 in name of G. Wilson had been completely omitted from the books.

(e) A provision of £24 for expenses accrued at 30 September Year 1 debited to General Expenses Account at that date had not been brought forward to the credit of the account in the following period and no credit entry had been made in any other account.

You are required:

(1) to prepare Journal Entries, with full narrations, to correct these errors;

(2) to write up the Difference Suspense Account;

(3) to prepare a statement showing the amended net profit for the year.

(C.A.)

Suggested Solution:

IN THE BOOKS OF CARELESS & COMPANY

(1)   JOURNAL

Year 2

Sept. 30			
Difference Suspense **Dr.**	£207	
To Sundries Unposted		£207

Being the inclusion of Bank Overdraft in Trial Balance previously unrecorded

Note: The credit is not made in the Cash Book since the balance is already recorded. To complete the journal entry the amount is shown as "Sundries Unposted" as no credit entry posting is necessary

Baker **Dr.**	£9	
To Difference Suspense		£9

Being amount of posting error from Cash Book to Baker's Personal Account now corrected

Difference Suspense **Dr.**	£172	
To Discount Received		£172

Being correction of posting error from Cash Book to Discount Received Account

Discount Allowed **Dr.**	£90	
To Difference Suspense		£90

Being correction of posting error from Cash Book to Discount Allowed Account

Difference Suspense **Dr.**	£24	
To General Expenses		£24

Being the balance brought forward at 30 Sept. Year 1 at credit of General Expenses Account now incorporated in the latter account

G. Wilson **Dr.**	£148	
To Sales		£148

Being inclusion of credit sale on Sept. 25 to G. Wilson in books previously omitted

(2)   *Difference Suspense Account*

Year 2 Sept. 30			Year 2 Sept. 30		
Sundries Unposted	£207		Balance	£304
Discount Received	172		Baker	9
General Expenses	24		Discount Allowed	90
	£403			£403

(3)   *Statement showing Amended Profit*

Profit per draft accounts before adjusting for errors	£3,600
Add: Adjustment to Discount Received Account	172
Additional sale to G. Wilson	148
Credit balance on General Expenses Account	24
	£3,944
Less: Adjustment to Discount Allowed Account	90
Amended Net Profit for year to 30 Sept. Year 2	£3,854

Examination Questions

Question 1

From the following information set out the Bank Reconciliation at 31 December Year 4 of Brown and Black:

(a) Balance due to bank at 31 December Year 4 per bank certificate £150.

(b) The following cheques were issued in December Year 4 but were not debited by the bank until January Year 5, £230; £12; £30,

(c) The firm was advised by the bank that a cheque for £50 lodged on 19 December had been dishonoured. No adjustment for this has been made in the firm's records.

(d) A lodgment for £450 was made on 31 December Year 4 but not credited by the bank until 2 January Year 5.

(e) The bank has been paying £2 per month under a standing order No. entries have been made in the firm's books for twelve months.

(f) Cash in bank per cash book at 31 December Year 4 amounts to £102.

Question 2

From the following information draw up a Bank Reconciliation Statement reconciling the two figures and show the cash book balance:

(a) Balance per bank statement on 31 December Year 6, £620 overdrawn.

(b) Commission amounting to £10 had been charged by the bank but was not shown in the cash book.

(c) Lodgment made on 31 December amounting to £600 was not credited by the bank until 2 January Year 7.

(d) A customer, R. Torr, had paid £50 direct to the bank and this had not been recorded in the cash book.

(e) Cheques drawn before 31 December Year 6 and not yet paid by the bank were as follows:

J. Brown	£90
R. Smith	£55
H. Bell	£49

(f) A quarterly payment of £100 to a Hire Purchase Company was made under a Banker's Order but the last four payments had not been recorded in the cash book.

Question 3

The cash book of J.N., a trader, showed a balance of £970 at the bank on 30 September Year 4.

On investigation you will find that:

(a) Cheques from customers amounting to £386 which were entered in the cash book on 30 September Year 4, were not credited by the bank until the following day.

(b) Cheques by J.N. on 29 September Year 4, £618, in favour of trade creditors, entered in the cash book on that day, were paid by the bank in October.

(c) On 17 August Year 4, a cheque for £196 was received from a customer and discount of £4 was allowed. £200 had been entered in the bank column of the cash book and credited to the customer. No entry for the discount was made in the books.

(d) In accordance with a standing order from J.N., the bank had paid £18 for a trade subscription on 30 September Year 4, but no entry had been made in J.N.'s books. The subscription is in respect of the year to 30 September Year 5.

(e) On 21 September Year 4, a credit transfer of £64, in settlement of the balance in a customer's account, was received by the bank for the credit of J.N., but no entry had been made in J.N.'s books.

(f) On 21 September Year 4, a cheque for £120 was received from a customer in settlement of his account and correctly entered in the books. This cheque was dishonoured and, on 26 September, the bank debited J.N.'s account, but no entry was made in J.N.'s books. It is considered that nothing will be recovered from this customer.

You are required to prepare:

(i) A statement showing the balance which should appear in the cash book on 30 September Year 4, after making all necessary corrections.

(ii) A statement showing your calculation of the balance shown by the bank statement on 30 September.

(iii) A statement reconciling the corrected cash book balance with the balance shown by the bank statement.

(iv) A statement showing your calculation of the correct net profit for the year to 30 September Year 4, assuming that the profit and loss account, before making any adjustments that may be required for the above matters, showed a net profit of £5,000.

(C.I.S.)

Question 4

You are required to enter the following items in the Petty Cash Book, using separate columns for (a) Postages; (b) Stationery; (c) Office Expenses.

May 1	Petty Cash in Hand	£25
5	Bought Envelopes	2
7	Bought Stamps	5
8	Bought Tea and Sugar	1
10	Bought Copy Paper	3
15	Bought Stamps	4
17	Bought Pens and Pencils	1
19	Bought Cleaning Materials	2
24	Bought Stamps	1
31	Bought Carbons	4

Balance the Petty Cash Book as at 31 May.

Question 5

A limited company has adopted the imprest system for petty cash. The amount of the imprest is £50 and the petty cashier is reimbursed on the first day of each calendar month with an appropriate amount of cash drawn from the bank.

On 31 December Year 4, the balance of petty cash in hand was £8. During the first three months of Year 5, the payments out of petty cash were:

January	£36
February	£48
March	£41

All payments from petty cash are charged to sundry expenses account.

Set out a summary of the petty cash account, in the Company's ledger, for the three months to 31 March Year 5, bringing down the balance at the end of each month.

(C.I.S.)

Question 6

Rule a Petty Cash account with appropriate columns, for the following items. The book is kept on the imprest system, the amount of the imprest being £30.

Jan.	1	Received from Cashier	£30 for Petty Cash
	3	Paid Travelling Expenses	3
	5	Bought Postage Stamps	1
	8	Paid Repairs to Typewriter	2
	10	Bought Envelopes	3
	15	Bought Stamps	1
	18	Paid Bus Fares	1
	20	Received in cash from A. Smith, a Debtor, in settlement of his account	10
	22	Paid for Shorthand Notebooks	4
	25	Paid Carriage	2
	27	Paid Parcel Post Charges	1
	28	Paid Taxi	2
	29	Paid office sundry expenses	1
	30	Paid Travelling Expenses	5
	31	Paid office cleaning expenses	4
		Paid R. Brown, Creditor, in cash in settlement of his account	6

Balance the Petty Cash Book as at 31 January and bring down the balance.

Question 7

Show by means of Journal Entries how you would record the following:

Jan. 4 The correction for £10 repairs to motor van posted to the debit of Motor Vehicles Account.

6 The purchase of a motor van on credit from Van Suppliers Ltd., £800.

8 Discount shown as £60 on the credit side of the cash book posted to the wrong side of the Discount Account.

10 Sale of a secondhand van to Motor Dealers Ltd., £150.

12 The correction for an undercast in the Sales Day Book of £20. The total sales should have been £1,050 not £1,030.

15 Discount deducted on payment of J. Smith's Account £3 has been disallowed by him.

18 £50 has been included in Wages Account and £100 in Purchases Account in respect of an extension to the office premises.

Question 8

Draw up the Journal entries to record the following transactions in the books of Jack Johnson, a sole trader:

(a) Johnson takes goods, costing £29, for his personal use.
(b) Simon Small owes Johnson £37. The debt has been outstanding for a considerable time and it is decided to treat it as a bad debt.
(c) Goods sold on credit to William Watson, amounting to £31, have been correctly entered in the Sales Day Book but have been entered, in error, in the Ledger Account of Walter Williams. Correct the error.
(d) Prepare the Journal entry necessary to transfer the following balances to Johnson's Trading Account at the end of the year.

Purchases	£4,763	Stock at commencement	
Sales	£6,994	of year	£1,059
Returns Inwards	£108	Stock at end of year	£1,201

(L. Ch. of C.)

Question 9

The Trial Balance extracted from the books of John Jones, a sole trader, at the close of business on 30 June Year 7 does not agree. The difference in the Trial Balance is entered in a Suspense Account and the Trading and Profit and Loss Accounts for the year ending 30 June Year 7 are then prepared. The net profit as shown in the Profit and Loss Account was £1,724.
Early in July Year 7 the following errors are discovered and these account for the differences in the Trial Balance.

(a) The Sales Day Book was undercast by £60.
(b) The cost of a new office desk had been debited in error to Wages Account. The amount was £34.
(c) The total discount allowed (£22) as shown in the Cash Book had been entered on the wrong side of Discount Account.
(d) Bad Debts Account had been debited £19 on 30 June in respect of a debt due from Arthur Armstrong but no credit entry had been passed.

From the above you are required to:

(i) draw up Journal Entries to correct the errors and
(ii) draw up a statement to show your calculations of the correct Net Profit.

(L. Ch. of C.)

Question 10

After draft accounts had been prepared for D. Maxwell, a sole trader, for the year ended 31 March Year 6, the following points arise:

(i) Maxwell's Drawings Account included £80 for fuel oil which had been used in the business.

(ii) Repairs to premises included the cost of a new garage for the firm's van amounting to £400.

(iii) Rates on Maxwell's house totalling £75 had been paid with those due on the shop premises and debited to Rates Account.

(iv) £140 received from B. Basil had been credited to the account of B. Bertram in error.

(v) Salaries include £150 paid to Maxwell's wife for services to the firm.

(vi) Wages of shop assistants include an amount of £10 for one week's wages to an employee who spent the whole week on repairing and renovating the van.

(vii) £15 has been received from C. Holme in respect of a debt of £50 which had been written off as bad three years ago. The receipt was credited to a new account opened in the name of C. Holme.

(viii) No provision had been made for doubtful debts but Maxwell agrees that provision amounting to £500 ought to be made.

(ix) An invoice for £125 had been entered in the Purchases Day Book on 30 March Year 6, but the goods were not received until 2 April and had not, therefore, been included in stock.

You are required:

(a) to give Journal Entries as are necessary to record the above adjustments;

(b) to prepare a statement showing the effect of these adjustments on the profit for the year ended 31 March Year 6.

(C. of S.)

4 Depreciation

4.1 THE NECESSITY FOR PROVIDING DEPRECIATION

The subject of depreciation is probably the most discussed accounting problem and indeed often causes the most dissension among accountants. As various opinions are held by members of the accountancy profession recommendations have been made by the accounting bodies in an endeavour to rationalize the methods of depreciating fixed assets. The basic concept of depreciation from a financial accounting point of view is simply that an allocation of the cost of an asset based on its service life is charged against the income of the business. This charge is known as depreciation. Thus depreciation accounting is not a method of asset valuation but a system of apportioning the cost of fixed assets over operating periods.

Why is depreciation a charge against income? Since the service lives of assets such as plant and machinery, motor vehicles, and fixtures and fittings are limited this gives rise to the consideration, if not the actual necessity, to provide for this diminution in value. If the cost of depreciation of assets is not determined the measurement of profit or loss will be adversely affected since no charge is being made for the expense of using the assets during their service life. If the service lives of assets were limitless and the assets never became obsolete then the problem of providing for depreciation could be almost entirely disregarded. But this is not so and the service life of an asset may be limited by the following factors:

(a) Actual deterioration of the asset through wear and tear or the passage of time.
(b) Obsolescence.
(c) Inadequacy.

4.11 ACTUAL DETERIORATION OF THE ASSET

The first factor is possibly the easiest to appreciate since wear and tear must arise from constant use of the asset in the factory or office or from advancing age. Since wear and tear from operation varies directly with the volume of output the service life of a similar type fixed asset will differ from business to business due to the changing levels of output achieved by the asset in each business. Again the useful life of a fixed asset will be greatly influenced by the repair and maintenance standards adopted by the firm.

4.12 OBSOLESCENCE

The problem of providing for the depreciation of an asset due to obsolescence is much more difficult since this factor can arise from a number of reasons which cannot be accurately forecast by management. New inventions may come on the market rendering present equipment obsolete; change in demand for products may necessitate new plant to be installed in the factory; improved methods of production may require additional and more sophisticated equipment to obtain the full advantage of new industrial techniques. Since there have recently been such rapid advances in science and technology many businesses are finding that plant and machinery are becoming obsolete long before their normal service life has been reached thus creating difficulties in the accurate assessment of depreciation charges. It can readily be appreciated that depreciation through obsolescence has become and will continue to be a great problem to the accountancy profession than depreciation through normal deterioration. Although it has always been considered prudent to follow a consistent policy in the provision of depreciation, nevertheless, it is imperative that a constant review of depreciation policies must be carried out by management and, if necessary, changes made in the light of technical and economic changes in industry and commerce. Unless consideration is given to these problems depreciation charges will become totally unrealistic and valueless.

4.13 INADEQUACY

This factor arises through business expansion whereby the fixed asset, though still in good working condition and capable of operating for a longer period of time, is incapable of achieving the increased service demanded of it.

4.2 FACTORS TO BE TAKEN INTO CONSIDERATION IN DETERMINING THE DEPRECIATION CHARGE

The main objective in depreciation accounting is to allocate the cost of fixed assets less any residual value over the estimated life of the assets in a methodical and reasonable manner. Original cost, residual scrap or trade-in value, and estimated service life of the asset are the important factors in determining a depreciation charge. Are there any problems in obtaining this information? The original cost of the asset can be accurately assessed without much difficulty by referring to the invoice or other relevant data at the date of purchase. The residual value of the asset, on the other hand, cannot be so easily assessed and in many cases an arbitrary amount is taken which may involve a wide margin of error. Finally the service life of the asset must be estimated if a charge for depreciation is to be calculated. This is always a difficult assessment to make due to the many contributing factors affecting the useful life of the asset. It is usual, in practice, to overcome the obvious problems of arriving at a scientific formula which can be consistently applied to determine the service life of the asset, by accepting guidance and advice from the firm's technical staff and the manufacturers of the asset to establish what might be a reasonable service life of the asset measured either in terms of years, output, or hours of operating time.

4.3   METHODS OF DEPRECIATION

Just as the interpretation of the word depreciation gives rise to argument among accountants and economists, the methods of providing for depreciation are equally contentious. The student must be aware of the different methods described below and at the same time study the underlying principles and advantages and disadvantages of each one.

4.31   FIXED INSTALMENT METHOD

Under the fixed instalment method, also known as the 'straight line' method, the cost of the asset is reduced by equal annual instalments until it is completely written off at the end of a fixed number of years. The amount of depreciation to be written off each year is calculated by using the following formula:

$$\frac{\text{Cost of Asset less residual value}}{\text{Estimated life of the Asset in years}}$$

The principal advantages of this method are its basic simplicity and that the asset can be completely written off at the end of a determinable number of years. One disadvantage to this method is that assets do not usually depreciate by a similar amount each year and so by writing down the asset in fixed proportions of the cost each year the amount so charged may be disproportionate to its real loss in value. There is also the added difficulty of depreciating additions to assets, particularly plant and machinery, where no detailed plant registers are kept. This method may also be unacceptable if the depreciation charge is based on the use of the asset and usage is inconsistent from period to period.

Accounting Entries

> **Dr.** Profit and Loss Account
> **Cr.** Depreciation Provision Account or Asset Account with the amount of the depreciation charge.

Question

Plant is purchased in Year 1 for £8,000. It is estimated that the life of the plant will be 10 years, leaving no residual value. Depreciation has to be written off at the rate of 10% per annum on the fixed instalment method. Show the journal entries and the appropriate ledger accounts for Years 1 and 2.

Suggested Solution:

JOURNAL

Year 1	Profit and Loss **Dr.**	£800	
	To Plant Depreciation Provision		£800
	Being annual charge for depreciation		
Year 2	Profit and Loss **Dr.**	£800	
	To Plant Depreciation Provision		£800
	Being annual charge for depreciation		

LEDGER

Dr.   *Plant Account*   **Cr.**

Year 1	Bank	£8,000			

Plant Depreciation Provision Account

Year 1	Balance	£800	Year 1	Profit and Loss	£800
Year 2	Balance	£1,600	Year 2	Balance	800
				Profit and Loss	800
		£1,600			£1,600
			Year 3	Balance	£1,600

Notes: (*a*) The annual depreciation charge may be credited directly to the Plant Account each year and no Plant Depreciation Provision Account opened but the above form is considered to be better practice.

(*b*) At the end of Year 2 the value of the Plant will appear in the Balance Sheet thus:

Plant—At Cost	£8,000	
Less: Depreciation to date	1,600	
	———	£6,400

4.32 REDUCING BALANCE METHOD

In this method a fixed percentage is written off the diminishing value of the asset each year so reducing it to a nominal value at the end of its life. This method is commonly used in small businesses where inadequate records of capital assets are kept and it is difficult to obtain the original cost of each asset and the date of purchase.

A significant advantage of this method is that depreciation charges are high in the initial years and the repairs and maintenance costs light while in the later years when the repairs and maintenance costs tend to rise the depreciation charge decreases. Another advantage is that it is simple to operate and is useful as a method of depreciation when the life of the asset cannot be estimated with reasonable accuracy since the asset is never completely written off.

In using this method care must be taken to ensure that a sufficiently high percentage rate of depreciation is used so that the asset may be written down to a residual value within its life span.

Question

Plant is purchased in Year 1 for £8,000. Depreciation is to be written off at the rate of 10% per annum on the reducing balance method. Show the journal entries and appropriate ledger accounts for Years 1 and 2.

Suggested Solution:

JOURNAL

Year 1	Profit and Loss	**Dr.**	£800	
	To Plant			£800
	Being annual charge for depreciation			
	———			
Year 2	Profit and Loss	**Dr.**	£720	
	To Plant			£720
	Being annual charge for depreciation			

LEDGER

Dr.			*Plant Account*			Cr.
Year 1	Bank	£8,000	Year 1	Profit and Loss		£800
				Balance		7,200
		£8,000				£8,000
Year 2	Balance	£7,200	Year 2	Profit and Loss		720
				Balance		6,480
		£7,200				£7,200

Notes: (*a*) Under this method it is more usual to write off the depreciation in the asset account but it is still possible to open a Depreciation Provision Account to which the charge for depreciation may be credited. It must be remembered that if the illustrated form of presentation is used care must be observed to ensure that details of the original cost and date of purchase of the asset are retained together with the total depreciation written off so that the information required by the Companies Acts, in the case of the Accounts of a limited company, may be available.

(*b*) If the above method was adopted the value of Plant will appear in the Balance Sheet at the end of Year 2 as follows:

Plant—at end of Year 1   £7,200
   Less: Depreciation for year   720
                                 ——— £6,480

In the Accounts of a limited company the asset Plant will require to be shown at cost and the total depreciation written off to date deducted therefrom.

4.33   REVALUATION METHOD

This method is practicable for providing depreciation on small tools and sundry items of equipment of low value but is not to be recommended as a method of depreciation for high cost assets such as buildings, motor vehicles, heavy plant and machinery, etc. The principle applied is that the difference between the book value of the asset and the valuation placed on the asset at the end of the financial period is treated as depreciation. The value of the asset on hand is calculated by inventory procedures and an estimate of its cost taking into account the present condition of the asset.

Question

The book value of loose tools at the beginning of Year 2 was £1,000. During the year purchases of small tools amounted to £500 and were debited to the Loose Tools Account. At the end of Year 2 the value of the tools was estimated to be £1,300. Show the Loose Tools Account for Year 2 as it would appear in the Ledger.

Suggested Solution:

LEDGER

Dr.			Loose Tools Account			Cr.
Year 2	Balance	£1,000	Year 2	Profit and Loss (Depreciation)	£200	
	Bank	500		Balance	1,300	
		£1,500			£1,500	

Notes: (a) Should the valuation show an increase over the book value of the loose tools the appreciation may either be ignored or transferred to the credit of a Special Reserve Account.

(b) The balance on the Loose Tools Account would be shown as an asset in the Balance Sheet.

4.34 ANNUITY SYSTEM

In this method the cost of the asset which represents a capital investment is regarded as earning a fixed annual rate of interest. The interest is debited to the Asset Account and credited to an Interest Account. Depreciation is written off the asset at a fixed amount calculated with reference to actuarial tables so that the asset will be completely written off at the end of a fixed number of years. Under this system the amount of interest earned, since it is related to the annual written down value of the asset, will reduce each year as depreciation reduces the book value of the asset. Although this is scientific in its conception it is rarely used in practice due to the complexity of the calculations involved when additions take place to the Asset Account and also for the reason that there is an increasing charge to revenue each year since the interest earned decreases annually while the depreciation charge is constant. Although it is considered impracticable as a method of depreciation for such assets as plant and machinery, motor vehicles, etc., it has some merit as a method of writing down the value of a lease over a long number of years.

Question

A lease is purchased for £1,000 for a period of 5 years. Interest is to be charged at the rate of 5%. By depreciating the lease using the annuity method show the journal entries, including bank transactions, for the first year and the ledger entries in the Asset Account for the full term of the lease. It is found by referring to the actuarial tables that the lease will require to be depreciated by £231 per annum.

Suggested Solution:

JOURNAL

Year 1	Lease **Dr.**	£1,000	
	To Bank		£1,000
	Being purchase of lease with a term of 5 years		
	Lease **Dr.**	£50	
	To Interest		£50
	Being annual charge for interest on cost of lease at 5% per annum		
	Profit and Loss (Depreciation on lease) **Dr.**	£231	
	To Lease		£231
	Being annual charge for the depreciation of the lease		

LEDGER

Dr.   *Lease Account*   **Cr**

Year 1	Bank	£1,000	Year 1	Profit and Loss (Depreciation)	£23·
	Interest	50		Balance	81·
		£1,050			£1,05·
Year 2	Balance	819	Year 2	Profit and Loss	23
	Interest (5% × £819)	41		Balance	62
		£860			£86
Year 3	Balance	629	Year 3	Profit and Loss	23·
	Interest	31		Balance	42·
		£660			£66·

Dr.					Cr.
Year 4	Balance	429	Year 4	Profit and Loss	231
	Interest	22		Balance	220
		£451			£451
Year 5	Balance	220	Year 5	Profit and Loss	231
	Interest	11			
		£231			£231

Notes: (*a*) The annual charge for depreciation may be posted to a Depreciation Account before being subsequently written off to the Profit and Loss Account.

(*b*) Due to the approximation of the depreciation charge being to the nearest £ the amount of interest in Year 3 has been slightly increased to balance the Asset Account in Year 5. In solutions to examination questions such approximations, unless stated in the question, should not be used.

4.35 DEPRECIATION OR SINKING FUND METHOD

The main reason for creating a Sinking Fund is to provide cash necessary to replace an asset at the end of its service life. It will have been seen in the previous methods described that depreciation is provided for the diminution in the value of the asset and no provision made for accumulating cash for its eventual replacement. In business today replacement of high cost assets due to normal deterioration or obsolescence may cause a serious depletion in cash reserves unless adequate financial arrangements have previously been made. The depreciation or sinking fund method differs from the other methods in this essential, namely, that an amount of cash equal to the depreciation written off is annually invested outside the business and allowed to accumulate at compound interest so as to produce the required replacement cash at a predetermined date.

A fixed amount, known as the Sinking Fund Instalment, is charged to Profit and Loss Account annually and credited to a Depreciation Fund Account. An amount equal to the fixed annual sum of depreciation is then invested in fixed interest bearing securities outside the business, the bank being credited and a Depreciation Fund Investment Account debited.

Since the amount invested will earn interest, the interest received will be credited to the Depreciation Fund Account and reinvested in the Depreciation Fund Investment Account which will result in the balances of these accounts being equal in amount.

Accounting Entries used under this Method

1. **Dr.** Asset Account with the purchase price.
   Cr. Bank if paid for by cheque.
   Under this method the asset remains in the books at its original cost.
2. **Dr.** Profit and Loss Account with annual charge for depreciation.
   Cr. Depreciation Fund Account.
3. **Dr.** Depreciation Fund Investment Account with annual sum to be invested equal to depreciation written off in the first year only.
   Cr. Bank.
4. **Dr.** Bank with interest received on investment.
   Cr. Depreciation Fund Account.
5. **Dr.** Depreciation Fund Investment Account with annual sum to be invested plus the interest received in the previous year.
   Cr. Bank.
6.   At the end of the period for which the Sinking Fund is set up the closing entries are:
   Dr. Depreciation Fund Account with the total depreciation accumulated in the fund.
   Cr. Asset Account; and
   Dr. Bank with the proceeds from the realization of the investment.
   Cr. Depreciation Fund Investment Account.

Question

A machine costing £1,000 has a life of three years. The residual value of the machine is considered to be nil. A sinking fund is to be set up to provide for its replacement. Amounts are invested annually which earn interest at the rate of 5%. From the sinking fund tables it is calculated that the annual instalment to be invested is £317 (to the nearest £). You are required to show the main ledger accounts to record the entries for the three years. Assume the investment realized £1,000 at the end of three years and this amount was paid into the firm's bank account.

Suggested Solution:

LEDGER

Dr.		*Depreciation Fund Account*				Cr.
Year 1	Balance		£317	Year 1	Profit and Loss	£317

Dr.   **Cr.**

Year 2	Balance	£650	Year 2	Balance	£317
				Bank (Interest)	16
				Profit and Loss	317
		£650			£650
Year 3	Machine	£1,000	Year 3	Balance	£650
				Bank (Interest)	33
				Profit and Loss	317
		£1,000			£1,000

Depreciation Fund Investment Account

Year 1	Bank	£317	Year 1	Balance	£317
Year 2	Balance	317	Year 2	Balance	650
	Bank	333			
		£650			£650
Year 3	Balance	£650	Year 3	Bank	1,000
	Bank	350			
		£1,000			£1,000

Machine Account

Year 1	Bank	£1,000	Year 3	Depreciation Fund	£1,000

Notes: (a) To simplify the solution, calculations have been made to the nearest £. In examination problems usually such approximations are not permitted.

(b) The Depreciation Fund Account may be described as a Sinking Fund Account.

(c) In some problems, as in practice, the investments may not realize the same amount as shown in the books in which even a gain or loss on realization will take place and be transferred to a Reserve Account.

4.36 INSURANCE POLICY METHOD

This method is similar in concept to the Depreciation Fund or Sinking Fund method with the exception that instead of investing in securities an amount is paid in the form of a premium to an Insurance Company for the purchase of an endowment policy which becomes realizable at the time of replacement of the asset.

The advantage of this method over the Depreciation Fund method is that a fixed sum will be paid by the Insurance Company on maturity of the policy thus avoiding possible fluctuations in the investment market resulting in gains or losses on realization of the investment.

Accounting Entries if a Policy Account is Opened

1. **Dr.** Endowment Policy Account with annual premium paid.
   Cr. Bank.
2. **Dr.** Profit and Loss Account with amount of annual premium written off.
   Cr. Depreciation Fund Account.
3. **Dr.** Endowment Policy Account with interest for year.
   Cr. Depreciation Fund Account.

Question

A machine costing £2,000 has an expected service life of ten years. An endowment policy is taken out to provide for its replacement. The annual premium is £100 per annum. The surrender value of the policy is the total premiums paid, plus 5% compound interest. Show the entries in the relevant ledger accounts for the first three years.

Suggested Solution:

Dr.   *Machine Account*   Cr.

| Year 1 | Bank | £2,000 | | |

Depreciation Fund Account

Year 1	Balance	£105	Year 1	Profit and Loss	£100
				Endowment Policy (Interest at 5%)	5
		£105			£105
Year 2	Balance	£215	Year 2	Balance	105
				Profit and Loss	100
				Endowment Policy	10
		£215			£215

Dr.   **Cr.**

Year 3	Balance	£331	Year 3	Balance	£215
				Profit and Loss	100
				Endowment Policy	16
		£331			£331

Endowment Policy Account

Year 1	Bank	£100	Year 1	Balance	£105
	Depreciation Fund				
	(Interest at 5%)	5			
		£105			£105
Year 2	Balance	105	Year 2	Balance	£215
	Bank	100			
	Depreciation Fund	10			
		£215			£215
Year 3	Balance	£215	Year 3	Balance	£331
	Bank	100			
	Depreciation Fund	16			
		£331			£331

Notes: (*a*) It has been assumed that the premiums have been paid at the beginning of each year and interest has been calculated at the rate of 5% per annum commencing in Year 1.

(*b*) The charge for interest has been calculated to the nearest £ to simplify the solution.

(*c*) On maturity of the policy the amount of the proceeds will be credited to the Endowment Policy Account. The balance on the Depreciation Fund Account will be transferred to the asset account.

4.37 OTHER METHODS OF PROVIDING FOR DEPRECIATION

The Depletion Method

This method is most commonly used in dealing with wasting assets such as mines and quarries and the charge for depreciation is not related to time but to tonnage extracted. Depreciation is usually charged on the basis of a rate per ton of material extracted.

The Machine Hour System

This system is used to advantage if a costing system is in operation. The formula adopted to provide depreciation on this basis is as follows:

$$\frac{\text{Cost of Machine less residual scrap value}}{\text{Estimated total effective working hours of service life of machine}}$$

By using this formula an hourly rate of depreciation is calculated which can then be applied to the number of hours the machine has been in operation during the period under review. This method is based upon the concept that the reduction in service life varies directly by the actual use of the asset rather than on an annual basis.

Replacement and Renewals Basis

This cannot, of course, be strictly considered as a method of depreciation but rather as an alternative to any depreciation at all. Replacement of assets may be dealt with by charging the actual cost of replacement to revenue. When this basis is adopted no funds are set aside for renewal of assets as replacement is provided out of current revenue and treated as a charge in the Profit and Loss Account. The cost of the original asset remains in the Books at its initial cost. It is only prudent to consider using this method for the replacement of low cost assets with a relatively short life.

4.4   PLANT REGISTER

In businesses where items of plant are numerous it is advisable to keep some form of register in which details of plant in use may be recorded. Although not always necessary, it is usual to prepare a separate sheet for each item of plant purchased giving the type of information shown in Figure 1. This type of plant register can also be used to record the amount of depreciation written off each item of plant as shown in the specimen sheet. Other information may be incorporated in the plant register relating to servicing of machines, major overhauls, etc., thus making it a useful record of plant not only to the accountancy department but to other departments within the company.

4.5   ACCOUNTING ENTRIES FOR THE PURCHASE AND SALE OF FIXED ASSETS

The following problems deal with the technique of recording the purchase and sale of assets such as plant and machinery, motor vehicles, furniture and

fixtures, etc. A study of the problems should only be made after fully understanding the meaning of depreciation and the methods used to provide for
depreciation.

Question

Plant is shown at cost in the Balance Sheet of A. Ltd. at £8,000. The total
depreciation written off the plant on the reducing balance method at 10%
per annum is £2,500. On the last day of Year 12, an item of plant originally
purchased in Year 9 for £500 was sold for cash £240. You are required to
show these transactions in the books of A. Ltd. and also how they would
appear in the Profit and Loss Account and Balance Sheet in Year 12.

Note: No depreciation has yet been provided for Year 12.

Suggested Solution:

Dr.			*Plant Account*			Cr.
Year 12	Balance	£8,000	Year 12	Plant Disposal		£500
				Balance		7,500
		£8,000				£8,000
Year 13	Balance	£7,500				

		Plant Depreciation Account			
Year 12	Plant Disposal	£136	Year 12	Balance	£2,500
	Balance	2,878		Profit and Loss	514
		£3,014			£3,014
			Year 13	Balance	£2,878

		Plant Disposal Account			
Year 12	Plant	£500	Year 12	Plant Depreciation	£136
				Bank	240
				Profit and Loss	
				(Loss on Sale)	124
		£500			£500

MAKER	Steel Products Ltd		MAKERS NO.	2314	DATE	LOCATION	REF.	DATE	LOCATION	REF.
	Newtown									
SUPPLIER	Machine Distributors		DRAWING REF.	21/2						
	Oldtown									
INVOICE NO.	5120	GUARANTEE	12 months							
INVOICE DATE	3 Jan. YR. 5.		NEW / SECOND HAND							

FULL DESCRIPTION   Model 25, Grinding machine

		FIRST COST			RE–VALUATIONS	
				REFERENCES	DATE	
	Invoice price	£1000				
	Foundation					
	Erection					
	TOTAL	£1000				

DRIVE		EXPECTED LIFE	Five YEARS
		DEPRECIATION RATE	20 %

ADDITIONS (Enter Sales in Red)

DATE	INVOICE NO.	SUPPLIER	ITEM	Code	COST

LOCATION	DESCRIPTION	CATEGORY	WORKS NO.
Department B	Grinding Machine	31	215

1 2 3 4 5 6 7 8 9 10 11 12

FIGURE 1

DEPRECIATION—BALANCE SHEET VALUES

ORIGINAL COST (or Balance B/F.) £1000   £1000

DATE	ADDITIONS	%	Depreciation and Other Credits	Total Depreciation to Date	BALANCE SHEET
Year 5 Jan. 3		20	£200	£200	£800

FINAL COMPUTATIONS

Balance Remaining _____
Amount Realized on disposal _____
Balance written off or back _____

TAXATION VALUES

Capital Cost £1000   Investment Grants Nil   Net Capital Cost or (Balance B/F) £1000

YEAR	ADDITIONS Capital Cost	Grants % AMT	Net Capital Cost	ALLOWANCES Initial % AMT	ALLOWANCES Annual % AMT	WRITTEN DOWN VALUE
19.5/6	£1000		£1000	10 £100	20 £200	£700

Deduct pre 1946 Additional Allowances _____
Amount Unallowed at time of sale _____
Disposal Price or Original Net Cost whichever is Lower _____
Balancing Allowance or Charge _____

Figure 1—*contd.*

Profit and Loss Account (**Dr.**) (Extract Year 12)

Depreciation on Plant	£514
Loss on Sale of Plant	£124

Balance Sheet (Extract Year 12)

Plant—at Cost	£7,500	
Less: Depreciation to date	2,878	
	———	£4,622

Working Notes:

Calculation of Loss on Plant Sold

			Depreciation Written Off
Cost Year 9		£500	
Depreciation Year 9	10%	50	
		———	£50
		450	
Depreciation Year 10		45	
		———	45
		405	
Depreciation Year 11		41	
		———	41
		364	
Proceeds of Sale		240	
		———	———
	Loss	£124	£136

Note: No depreciation is required to be written off in the year of sale.

Depreciation Charge

Balance of Plant Account Year 12		£7,500
Less: Depreciation to Year 11	£2,500	
Less: Depreciation on plant sold	136	
	———	2,364
		£5,136
	at 10% p.a.	£514

The question opposite is a more difficult problem dealing with the purchase and sale of motor vehicles.

Question

In the Accounts of a Taxi Business which are made up to 31 December, depreciation has been provided at 25% of the reducing balance, a full year's charge being made for the year in which a taxi is bought.

The Balance Sheet as on 31 December Year 8, included:

Taxis at cost	£11,750
Less: Depreciation	5,996
	£5,754

It is decided to change the basis of calculation of the annual depreciation charge to 20% of cost on the Balance Sheet date and to amend the accumulated provision for depreciation as on 31 December Year 8 to one computed on this basis.

The fleet had been bought as follows:

During Year 4	£4,000
6	1,500
7	2,750
8	3,500
	£11,750

During Year 9 changes in the fleet were:

Sales	Proceeds	Date Bought	Cash
QTZ 611	£150	6 May Year 4	£900
STF 420	300	12 Mar. Year 6	950
WTA 191	650	12 June Year 7	1,000
			£2,850

Purchases	
ZTC 357	£1,000
ZTC 358	1,000
ZTC 359	1,000
	£3,000

In the nominal ledger, there are separate Accounts for the fleet at cost, depreciation, and profit and loss on sales.

You are required:

(a) to prepare schedules to show:
   (i) the additional depreciation provision required on the fleet on 31 December Year 8, for the past years resulting from the change of basis;
   (ii) the depreciation charge for Year 9; and
   (iii) the profit or loss on cars sold during Year 9, and
(b) to record these matters in the nominal ledger.

(C.A. E. & W. adapted)

Suggested Solution:

(a) (i) *Additional amount of depreciation to be written off under new depreciation basis*

New Basis—20% of Cost

Cost	Annual Charge	No. of Years	Total Depreciation
£4,000	800	5	£4,000
1,500	300	3	900
2,750	550	2	1,100
3,500	700	1	700
			£6,700

Total Depreciation charge under new basis	£6,700
Total Depreciation charge under old basis	£5,996
Additional amount to be written off	£704

(ii) *Calculation of Annual Charge for Depreciation for Year 9*

	Total	Year 4	Year 6	Year 7	Year 8	Year 9
Cost	£11,750	4,000	1,500	2,750	3,500	
Purchased in Year 9	3,000					3,000
	14,750					
Less: Sales in Year 9	2,850	900	950	1,000	—	—
As at 31 Dec. Year 9	11,900	3,100	550	1,750	3,500	3,000
Less: Depreciation in Year 9	£1,760	—	110	350	700	600

Total depreciation written off in Year 9 is £1,760

Note: No depreciation has been deducted from taxis acquired in Year 4 since the cost has been completely written off.

(iii) *Calculation of Profit or Loss on Sale of Taxis during Year 9*

		QTZ 611		STF 420		WTA 191	
Cost		£900		£950		£1,000	
Less: Depreciation written off to date	(5 × 180)	900	(3 × 190)	570	(2 × 200)	400	= £1,870
		—		380		600	
Sale Proceeds		150		300		650	
	Profit	£150	Loss	£80	Profit	50	

Total profit on sale of taxis in Year 9 is £120

(b)

IN THE NOMINAL LEDGER

Dr. *Taxis Account* **Cr.**

Year 9			Year 9		
Jan. 1	Balance	£11,750	Dec. 31	Taxis Disposal	£2,850
Dec. 31	Bank	3,000		Balance	11,900
		£14,750			£14,750
Year 10					
Jan. 1	Balance	£11,900			

Dr. *Taxis Depreciation Account* **Cr.**

Year 9			Year 9		
Dec. 31	Taxis Disposal	£1,870	Jan. 1	Balance	£5,996
	Balance	6,590	Dec. 31	Profit and Loss (additional depreciation)	704 ·
				Profit and Loss (annual depreciation)	1,760
		£8,460			£8,460
			Year 10		
			Jan. 1	Balance	£6,590

Taxis Disposal Account

Year 9			Year 9		
Dec. 31	Taxis	£2,850	Dec. 31	Taxis Depreciation	£1,870
	Profit and Loss	120		Bank (Proceeds of Sale)	1,100
		£2,970			£2,970

Examination Questions

Question 1

The balance appearing in the ledger for Plant and Machinery is £5,260 at 31 March Year 8.

This is made up as follows:

Cost		£8,000
Less: Depreciation	£2,500	
Proceeds of Sale of Machine	240	2,740
		£5,260

The machine which was sold during the year was purchased on 1 April Year 4 at a cost of £500. Depreciation has been written off Plant and Machinery at 10% per annum on the reducing balance method. No depreciation has yet been provided for Year 8.

You are required to calculate the gain or loss on the sale of the machine and show the amounts which would appear in the Balance Sheet for Plant and Machinery at 31 March Year 8.

Question 2

The following balances are shown in the books of Conveyors Ltd. at 31 March Year 6:

Proceeds of Sale of motor vehicle		£280
Motor Vehicles at cost	£3,052	
Total depreciation to 1 April Year 5	943	
		2,109

The figure for motor vehicles includes a new vehicle purchased on 1 December Year 5, for £600. The vehicle sold was purchased on 1 April Year 1, for £820. Depreciation on written down values has been provided annually for motor vehicles at 25%.

Give the entry for motor vehicles as it should appear in the Balance Sheet at 31 March Year 6, and show how you arrive at your figures. (Make calculations to the nearest £1.)

(A.C.C.A.)

Question 3

The Glenhome Transport Company purchased several vehicles as follows:

1 Jan. Year 5 —Purchased four vehicles Nos. 1–4 at £2,200 each
1 Jan. Year 6 —Purchased two vehicles Nos. 5 and 6 at £2,400 each
30 June Year 6—Sold vehicle No. 2 for £1,200

It was decided that depreciation should be credited to a separate account and that it should be written off each year at 31 December at the rate of 20% per annum on cost, account being taken of the period of use during the year.

You are required to write up the Asset Account, the Depreciation Account, and the Depreciation Provision Account for the Years 5 and 6 and to show how you would deal with the sale of vehicle No. 2 assuming that any profit or loss arising out of the sale is transferred to Profit and Loss Account.

The Company's financial year ends on 31 December.

Question 4

A. Carrier owned three lorries at 1 April Year 6, viz:

A purchased 21 May Year 2	Cost £1,560	
B purchased 20 June Year 4	,,	£980
C purchased 1 Jan. Year 6	,,	£2,440

Depreciation is taken at 20% of cost per annum, ignoring fractions of a year.

During the year to 31 March Year 7, the following transactions occurred:

   (1) 1 June Year 6 B was involved in an accident and considered a write off by the Insurance Company who paid £525 compensation.
   (2) 7 June Year 6 D was purchased for £1,640.
   (3) 21 Aug. Year 6 A was sold for £350
   (4) 30 Oct. Year 6 E was purchased for £1,950.
   (5) 6 Mar. Year 6 E was not considered suitable for carrying the type of goods required and was exchanged for F. The value of F was considered to be £1,880.

You are required to show the accounts to record these transactions, including the depreciation charge for the year to 31 March Year 7, in Carrier's books.

(A.C.C.A.)

Question 5

The vehicles and plant register of Hexagon Transport Ltd. shows the following vehicles in service at 30 September Year 8:

	ABC	DEF	GHJ	KLM	NOP
Registration No.	242	108	832	23	666
Purchased during the year ended 30 Sept.	Year 4	Year 5	Year 6	Year 7	Year 8
Original Cost	£800	£860	£840	£950	£980

Up to 30 September Year 8, the company had depreciated its major vehicles by 20% per annum on the diminishing balance system, but as from 1 October Year 8 it is decided to adopt the straight-line method of depreciation and to write all the vehicles down to an estimated residual value of £20 each over an estimated life of five years. The company wishes to adjust the accrued depreciation provisions on the existing vehicles in line with this policy.

During the year ended 30 September Year 9 the company has purchased vehicle QRS 913 for £960 and sold DEF 108 for £60.

A whole year's depreciation is provided for every vehicle on hand at the end of any accounting period.

You are required to:

  (a) Reconstruct the entries for each vehicle in the register, as it appeared on 30 September Year 8.
  (b) Calculate the necessary adjustments to be made in respect of the depreciation provisions on 1 October Year 8.

(c) Complete the entries in the register for the year to 30 September Year 9 showing clearly how you calculate any adjustment necessary in respect of the sale of DEF 108.

Calculations to be made to the nearest £.

(I.C.W.A. adapted)

Question 6

From the following information prepare the Motor Vehicle Account, the Motor Vehicle Depreciation Account, and the Gain or Loss on Realization of Vehicles Account as they would appear in the Nominal Ledger of Down Enterprises Limited at 28 February Year 9.

1. At 29 February Year 8, the balance on Motor Vehicles Account and Motor Vehicles Depreciation Account were £5,720 and £3,725 respectively.
2. During the year there were the following transactions in motor vehicles:

Year 8

Apr. 30	Morris Car purchased	£800
Aug. 1	Bedford van sold (originally purchased in May Year 4 for £800)	£200
Dec. 1	Vauxhall car, allowance given on part exchange for Ford car (Vauxhall originally purchased in Jan. Year 2 for £900)	£100
Dec. 1	Cash paid for Ford purchased	£600

3. Annual depreciation is calculated at 25% of the net book value of the motor vehicles at the end of each financial year.

(C.A.)

Question 7

The following balances appeared in the Books of B. Ltd. at 1 January Year 5:

Freehold Property	£46,000	
Plant and Machinery	75,304	
Motor Vehicles	16,200	
Depreciation:		
Freehold Property		£3,450
Plant and Machinery		35,230
Motor Vehicles		10,700

During the year ended 31 December Year 5, the following transactions took place:

(a) Capital expenditure totalling £33,350 was incurred, made up of:

> Freehold Property £6,000; Plant and Machinery £22,350; Motor Vehicles £5,000

(b) Plant purchased in Year 1 for £4,000 was scrapped and plant purchased in Year 2 for £1,100 was sold for £350.

(c) Motor vehicles purchased in Year 2 for £10,666 were sold for £5,100.

Depreciation has been calculated, without adjustment for the number of months applicable to particular assets, at the following rates since the Company was incorporated:

Freehold Property	$2\frac{1}{2}\%$ on original cost
Plant and Machinery	10% on written down value at the year end
Motor Vehicles	25% on written down value at the year end

You are required to show:

(a) The entries relating to Fixed Assets and Depreciation as they would appear in the Balance Sheet at 31 December Year 5.

(b) The depreciation charge for the year ended 31 December Year 5 as it would appear in the Profit and Loss Account.

(c) The calculations of the Fixed Asset balances and the charge for depreciation.

(I.C.W.A.)

5 Capital and Revenue Expenditure

5.1 CAPITAL EXPENDITURE

Capital expenditure can be described as expenditure incurred in acquiring assets of a permanent nature, the benefit of which extends over one or more accounting periods. An expenditure of this type which is charged to an Asset Account is considered to be capitalized. Examples of capital expenditure are land and buildings, plant and machinery, motor vehicles, furniture and fittings, additions and extensions to existing assets. Capital expenditure is not charged to the Profit and Loss Account but the reduction in value of those assets having a limited life is written off by way of depreciation to the latter account.

5.2 REVENUE EXPENDITURE

Revenue expenditure is so termed when the benefits do not extend beyond the accounting period in which the expenditure takes place. This form of expenditure is recorded in the appropriate Expense Accounts and written off at the end of each accounting period in the Trading and Profit and Loss Account. Such expenditure does not increase the value of the fixed assets of the business but services and maintains them in good working condition. The costs of producing, selling, and distributing the goods and services of the business together with the administration expenses involved are also examples of revenue expenditure. Purchases, wages, salaries, commission, rent, rates, electricity, telephone, printing and stationery are expenses of a revenue nature. In some businesses expenditure which would normally fall into the category of capital expenditure may be treated as revenue expenditure, for practical purposes, if the expenditure is relatively small, say under £20, or where there is no significant or measurable benefit accruing to a future period.

5.3 NECESSITY TO DISTINGUISH BETWEEN CAPITAL AND REVENUE EXPENDITURE

In general terms the distinction between capital and revenue expenditure is one of permanence. In other words, what is the duration of benefit accruing from the outlay of the expenditure? It is essential that a distinction be drawn between capital and revenue expenditure if a true and correct revenue profit or loss is to be computed. Revenue profit earned by a business is calculated by deducting the total revenue expenditure including depreciation charges from the gross income received. If any capital expenditure is included in this calculation a false revenue profit or loss will result. Only expenditure such as the actual revenue expenses of operating the business may be charged to the Trading and Profit and Loss Accounts. The diminution in the value of any of the fixed assets may be charged to the Profit and Loss Account in the form of a depreciation provision.

Although an attempt has been made to establish rules to differentiate between capital and revenue expenditure it does not always follow that each item of expenditure must always be classified as being capital or revenue expenditure. If a firm uses its own employees to erect an extension to its factory premises then it would be incorrect to treat the amount of wages paid to the firm's own employees engaged in this work as revenue expenditure together with the cost of any materials used in the construction of the premises. This expenditure must be treated as capital expenditure since it is not part of the cost of producing goods for resale but relates directly to the cost of acquiring a capital asset in the form of additional factory premises. Legal expenses, provided they are incurred in the collection of bad debts or for a similar reason, are written off as revenue expenditure but if they are paid in respect of acquiring additional assets or the raising of capital they are considered to be capital expenditure and treated accordingly in the financial accounts. The title of the expense item does not of itself determine its correct allocation and consequently a careful assessment of each cost item must be made before it is classified as capital or revenue expenditure.

Question

You are required to allocate the following items of expenditure between capital and revenue:

(a) Replacement typewriter purchased by the office.
(b) Materials purchased but used for the erection of a new office block for the firm's use.

(c) Fitting replacement engine to a delivery van.
(d) Development costs in opening a new mine.
(e) Purchase of patent rights.
(f) Cost of hiring a motor van.
(g) Installation charges in connection with new oil-fired boiler replacing coal fires.
(h) Cleaning and greasing new machine.
(i) Painting and lettering new delivery van.
(j) Legal fees in connection with mortgage on property.

Suggested Solution:

(a) Capital   (f) Revenue
(b) Capital   (g) Capital
(c) Revenue   (h) Revenue
(d) Capital   (i) Capital
(e) Capital   (j) Capital

Question

George and Harry Black are in partnership as agricultural engineers. In their nominal ledger they maintain the usual accounts for fixed assets and also repairs equalization accounts for buildings and plant, to which annual charges of £150 and £1,000 respectively are credited.

The following balances appear on these accounts at 1 June:

Land and Buildings	£10,720
Plant and Equipment	17,800
Motor Vehicles	3,600
Building repairs equalization account	412 (**Cr.**)
Plant, etc., repairs equalization account	27 (**Dr.**)

(a) Complete the above ledger accounts for the year ended 31 May and include such of the following items as are relevant:

(i) Purchase of additional land and buildings at 47 Front Street:

Purchase price	£6,750	
Legal Charges	104	
Rates paid in advance by vendor	17	
		£6,871

(ii) Purchase of Motor Van XYZ 606:

Basic cost	£615	
Delivery charge	8	
Number plates	4	
Road Fund Tax	15	
		£642

(iii) Lettering the firm's name on Van XYZ 606	£24
(iv) Partial demolition of 47 Front Street	£319

(v) Builder and decorator's account for 47 Front Street:

Erection of new office block	£2,500	
Alterations to the original structure	750	
Painting and general repairs	375	
		£3,625

(vi) Purchase of water heater for new office	£20
(vii) Installation of water heater in new office	£18

(viii) Purchase of 'Digsworth' lathe on hire purchase terms:

Cash price of lathe	£3,700
Deposit	925
Interest charges over two years	444

(ix) Cost of installing the 'Dogsworth' lathe	£125
(x) Costs of re-positioning the existing plant to accommodate the 'Dogsworth' lathe	£375

Other expenditure during the year was:

Plant repairs	£847
Building repairs	214

(b) If you feel that the correct treatments of any of the items are debatable add *brief* notes supporting the methods you suggest.

(I.C.W.A.)

Suggested Solution:

(a)

Dr.	Land and Buildings Account					Cr.
June 1	Balance	£10,720	May 31	Balance		£21,143
June 1– May 31	Bank—Land, 47 Front Street	6,750				
	Bank—Legal Charges	104				
	Bank—Partial demoli- tion of 47 Front Street	319				
	Bank—Erection of new office block	2,500				
	Bank—Alteration to original structure	750				
		£21,143				£21,143
June 1	Balance	£21,143				

	Plant and Equipment Account					
June 1	Balance	£17,800	May 31	Balance		£22,038
June 1– May 31	Bank—Water Heater	20				
	Bank—Installation of Water Heater	18				
	Hire Vendor—Cash price of lathe	3,700				
	Bank—Installation of lathe	125				
	Bank—Re-position- ing existing plant	375				
		£22,038				£22,038
June 1	Balance	£22,038				

	Motor Vehicles Account					
June 1	Balance	£3,600	May 31	Balance		£4,251
June 1– May 31	Bank—Basic Cost of XYZ 606 plus deliv- ery charges and number plates	627				
	Bank—Cost of letter- ing	24				
		£4,251				£4,251
June 1	Balance	£4,251				

Dr.	*Building Repairs Equalization Account*				Cr.
June 1– May 31	Bank—Painting and General Repairs Bank—Building Repairs	375 214	June 1 May 31	Balance Profit and Loss Balance	412 150 27
		£589			£589
June 1	Balance	£27			

	Plant Repairs Equalization Account				
June 1 June 1– May 31	Balance Bank—Plant Repairs Balance	27 847 126	May 31	Profit and Loss	1,000
		£1,000			£1,000
			June 1	Balance	£126

(*b*) *Notes supporting methods used.* 1 The cost of the water heater in the office together with the cost of installation would normally be debited to the Office Fixtures and Fittings Account

2. The cost of partial demolition of 47 Front Street is treated as capital expenditure since it is considered as the cost of preparing the site for the new office block

3. The costs of repositioning the existing plant are treated as capital expenditure since the benefit accruing from the re-siting of the plant would be on a long-term basis.

4. The initial cost of lettering the van is treated as capital expenditure but any repainting or relettering of the van would be revenue expenditure. On the other hand the road fund tax of the new vehicle is considered revenue expenditure since it is a cost of running the vehicle, the value of which is used up in the year.

5. Only the cash price of the 'Dogsworth' lathe is debited to the Plant and Equipment Account. The interest charges are written off to Profit and Loss Account over the term of the H.P. Agreement.

Additional Notes

Building Repairs Equalization Account and Plant Repairs Equalization Account

The purpose of opening the above equalization accounts is to attempt to eliminate the fluctuation of the annual charge for building and plant repairs in the final accounts. This is achieved by deciding on a fixed amount to be charged annually to the Profit and Loss Account in respect of building and plant repairs. This fixed charge is calculated as an average amount taking into account past and anticipated expenditure for those repairs. All expenditure during the year for those items is debited to the relevant equalization account. Any balance arising after the annual fixed charge is entered in the equalization account is carried forward to the next financial year. The balances on these accounts, if any, will be shown in the Balance Sheet.

Examination Questions

Question 1

Explain the basic principles which would guide you in allocating expenditure as between capital and revenue.

(Com. A.)

Question 2

On what principles would you distinguish between capital and revenue expenditure in the following cases:

(*a*) Replacement of a motor vehicle which originally cost £750 but which has been depreciated 20% per annum on cost for four years and eventually sold for £20, by a new vehicle costing £1,100.
(*b*) Repairs and extensions of premises.
(*c*) Loss of stock by fire amounting to £4,000 and a receipt of £3,200 in full settlement from the Insurance Company.

(Com. A.)

Question 3

Distinguish the following items between capital and revenue expenditure:

(*a*) Cost of cementing car park at rear of factory.
(*b*) Legal fees on land purchased for factory extension.
(*c*) Factory foreman's salary supervising construction of extension to factory.
(*d*) Cost of overhauling factory machinery.
(*e*) Painting existing factory building.

(*f*) Cost of removing power machines from existing factory to factory extension and resetting them in concrete £500.

(*g*) Accountants' Fees agreeing taxation liability of company.

(*h*) Auditor's Fees re annual audit of company's books.

(*i*) Cash stolen from safe by junior clerk £30.

6 Bills of Exchange and Cheques

6.1 INTRODUCTION

The passing of the Bills of Exchange Act, 1882, codified the law relating to Bills of Exchange, Cheques, and Promissory Notes. This act has been slightly amended from time to time by the passing of further legislation, a recent change being the Cheques Act, 1957. As it is not possible, nor is it intended, to discuss in this chapter all the provisions in the Bills of Exchange Act, 1882, and the subsequent amending acts, the reader is advised to study the various acts affecting Bills of Exchange to become familiar with the legal aspects of this topic.

Bills of Exchange may be divided into two main groups:

(*a*) Inland Bills.
(*b*) Foreign Bills.

An Inland Bill is a bill which on the face of it purports to be (*a*) both drawn and payable within the British Isles or (*b*) drawn within the British Isles upon some person resident therein. All other bills are considered to be Foreign Bills.

6.2 DEFINITION OF A BILL OF EXCHANGE

A Bill of Exchange, as defined by the Bills of Exchange Act, 1882, is an unconditional order in writing, addressed by one person to another, signed by the person giving it, requiring the person to whom it is addressed to pay on demand or at a fixed or determinable future time a sum certain in money to or to the order of a specified person or to bearer. An instrument which does not comply with these conditions, or which orders any act to be done in addition to the payment of money, is not a bill of exchange.

It is important to appreciate that a bill establishes a debt between two parties. In the first instance the drawer by signing the bill acknowledges that the drawee owes the amount shown on the face of the bill and by accepting it the drawee agrees that he is liable to pay the sum stated and that he will honour his obligation on maturity of the bill.

Bills of Exchange, like cheques and promissory notes, are known as negotiable instruments. This means that, unless it is stated to be not negotiable, the rights conferred by the bill of exchange can be passed by delivery of the bill to another person who, if he receives it in good faith, obtains a complete and absolute title to it free from any defect in the transferor's title.

6.21 PARTIES TO A BILL OF EXCHANGE

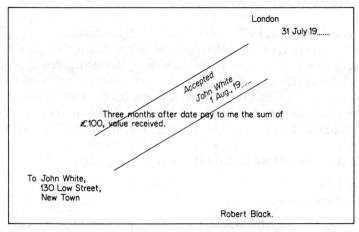

FIGURE 2

Figure 2 is a specimen Bill of Exchange. The following definitions relate to some of the principal parties involved in bills.

Drawer   Robert Black, the person who has drawn and signed the above bill, is known as the Drawer and to whom it is a Bill Receivable.

Drawee   John White is the person on whom the Bill is drawn and is referred to as the Drawee.

Acceptor   John White becomes the acceptor when he signs the bill acknowledging his acceptance of it. The acceptance is made on the face of the bill although the word 'accepted' is not always included. To White this is a Bill Payable.

Payee   The payee is the party to whom payment is to be made. Usually the payee and the drawer are the same, as is the case in the specimen bill of exchange. This need not always be the position. The wording on the bill of exchange may be as follows:

'Three months after date pay to Ronald Sime or order the sum of £100, value received.'

In this bill the drawer and the payee will be different persons.

Endorser An endorser is the person who holds a bill payable to order and endorses it by writing his name on the back of it. The negotiation of the bill is then completed by delivery.

Holder and Holder in due course A holder means the payee or endorser of a bill or note who is in possession of it, or the bearer thereof. On the other hand a holder in due course is a holder who has taken a bill, complete and regular on the face of it, under the following conditions, viz. that he became the holder of it before it was overdue, and without notice that it had been previously dishonoured, if such was the fact; and that he took the bill in good faith and for value, and that at the time the bill was negotiated to him he had no notice of any defect in the title of the person who negotiated it.

6.22 ADVANTAGES OF USING A BILL OF EXCHANGE

(a) The debtor by accepting a bill of exchange is able to obtain a fixed period of credit from his creditor.

(b) The creditor by drawing up a bill of exchange and obtaining acceptance from his debtor is in possession of legal evidence of the debt and a fixed date of payment.

(c) The creditor may, if he so wishes, discount the bill with his bank and so obtain funds without waiting until the bill matures.

(d) Since a bill of exchange is a negotiable instrument it can be transferred to another party in settlement of the customer's debt.

(e) It is a means of settling foreign debts and enabling the exporter to obtain money from his banker.

6.23 DISHONOURING A BILL

A bill is considered to be dishonoured by non-payment when it has been duly presented for payment and payment is refused or cannot be obtained. When a bill is dishonoured on presentation in this way an immediate right of recourse against the drawer and endorsers accrues to the holder, but notice of dishonour must be given to the drawer and each endorser or they may be discharged from their obligations. In certain circumstances the bill may be handed to a Notary Public who presents the bill for payment and then certifies that the bill has been presented in time at the correct place and it has been dishonoured. This is referred to as noting a bill for non-payment and may be followed by another formal act known as protest. The Notary's fees for his services in this connection are the responsibility of the holder of the bill who in turn may charge the costs to the acceptor or to the party from whom he received the bill.

6.24 DISCOUNTING A BILL

A bill of exchange may be discounted at a bank thus enabling a trader to obtain funds which he may immediately require for meeting financial commitments before the bill reaches maturity. In most cases the banker will discount the bill less a sum of discount, the amount of which depends on the time the bill is payable and the discount rate ruling at that time. By discounting the bill with his banker the drawer is not relieved of his financial responsibility to the banker, in the case of the bill being dishonoured, when presented for payment. In these circumstances he has to repay the amount of the bill to the bank plus any charges incurred by the bank.

6.25 RENEWING A BILL

If the acceptor of a bill realizes that he will be unable to meet his obligation regarding payment on maturity of the bill he may by agreement with the drawer request that the bill be renewed for a further period of time. If the drawer accedes to this request a new bill will be drawn up usually with an amount of interest added to it in compensation for the delay in settlement together with any additional costs incurred by the drawer. The original bill which is being replaced with the new one will be cancelled and the appropriate accounting entries recorded in the books of both parties.

6.26 ACCOMMODATION BILL

An Accommodation Bill is a bill which has been drawn up, accepted, or endorsed, for the express purpose of enabling a person to raise money by discounting it although no value has been received. It is the fact that no value has been received which makes this form of bill different from the type used n normal trading transactions. The accounting procedure in the recording of Accommodation Bills is the same as in the case of ordinary bills but it is important to note that the discount charges fall to be charged against the party or parties accommodated usually in proportion to the extent of the accommodation enjoyed by each party.

5.27 DAYS OF GRACE

Three days called days of grace are, in every case unless the bill is payable on demand, added to the time of payment as fixed by the bill, and the bill is due and payable on the last day of grace. If the last day of grace falls on a Sunday, Christmas Day, or Good Friday, the bill is due and payable on the preceding day. On the other hand if the last day of grace is a bank holiday (with the exception of Christmas Day or Good Friday) it is due and payable on the succeeding business day.

5.3 BILL BOOKS

When the number of bills becomes numerous it is advisable to open subsidiary books known as Bills Receivable Book and Bills Payable Book. Those books enable a record to be kept of the various particulars relating to the bills and may be used as a posting medium to the Bill Accounts in the ledger. Overleaf are specimen rulings of bill books showing the type of information which may be recorded in such books. The rulings, of course, may be varied to suit the requirements of individual businesses.

5.4 PROMISSORY NOTES AND CHEQUES

Mention has been made earlier in this chapter that the Bills of Exchange Act, 1882, was passed to codify the law not only relating to bills of exchange but also to promissory notes and cheques. It is not intended to deal at great length with promissory notes and cheques but it is important to note the definitions of these terms as stated in the Bills of Exchange Act, 1882, and to appreciate the differences between them.

5.41 PROMISSORY NOTE

An unconditional promise in writing made by one person to another, signed by the maker, engaging to pay on demand or at a fixed or determinable

BILLS RECEIVABLE BOOK

No. of Bill	Date Received	From Whom Received	Drawer	Acceptor	Where Payable	Date of Bill	Term	Due Date	Ledger Folio	Amount	How Disposed Of
1	1 Jan.	R. Jones	Self	R. Jones	The Bank Old St., Newtown	1 Jan.	Four Months	4 May	21	£2,000	Discounted 1 Jan.

BILLS PAYABLE BOOK

No. of Bill	Date	To Whom Given	Drawer	Payee	Where Payable	Date of Bill	Term	Due Date	Ledger Folio	Amount	How Disposed Of
1	1 Jan.	T. Brown	T. Brown	T. Brown	The New Bank London	1 Jan.	Four Months	4 May	5	£1,000	Honoured

uture time a sum certain in money to, or to the order of, a specified person
r to bearer.

A promissory note is essentially a promise to pay made out by a debtor
nd is usually for a loan transaction. No acceptance is required and no
pecial wording is laid down by the Act.

.42 CHEQUE

A cheque is a bill of exchange drawn on a banker payable on demand.
Certain sections of the Act make special provision for presentment of cheques
or payment such as general and special crossing and revocation of banker's
uthority, but in the main the provisions of the Bills of Exchange Act, 1882,
pplicable to a bill of exchange apply to a cheque.

.5 CONTINGENT LIABILITY

f a bill of exchange which is receivable by a firm or company has been
iscounted there is still a liability on the part of the firm or company to the
anker discounting the bill, if the bill is not met on maturity. No accounting
ntry, however, is required to record this liability in the business books but
here is a statutory obligation, in accordance with the provisions of the Com-
anies Act, 1948, for companies to indicate this contingent liability, by way
f note, on the Balance Sheet issued to shareholders. There is, however, no
tatutory obligation to record this information in the Balance Sheet of a
artnership or sole trader.

.6 ACCOUNTING ENTRIES TO RECORD BILLS OF EXCHANGE

he accounting entries required to record Bills of Exchange in the books of
e acceptor and drawer, in journal and ledger form, are shown below.
urnal entries for bank transactions are also included.

61 ENTRIES IN THE BOOKS OF THE ACCEPTOR (JOHN WHITE) TO WHOM IT IS A BILL PAYABLE

) *On Acceptance of the Bill*

John White accepts the bill drawn on him by Robert Black at three months
r £100 being the amount due to Robert Black.

JOURNAL

Robert Black	**Dr.** £100	
To Bills Payable		£100

Being acceptance of bill at three months drawn by Robert Black.

LEDGER

Dr.   *Robert Black Account*   C

Bills Payable	£100	Balance	£10

Bills Payable Account

		Robert Black	£10

When the bill is accepted by John White he is required to transfer th
amount of the bill from Robert Black's Account to a Bills Payable Accour
thus reducing creditors and increasing bills payable.

(*b*) *On Honouring the Bill*

John White honours the bill at maturity.

JOURNAL

Bills Payable	**Dr.** £100	
To Bank		£100

Being settlement of bill drawn by Robert Black.

LEDGER

Dr.   *Bills Payable Account*   C

Bank	£100	Balance	£10

Bank Account

		Bills Payable	£10

On honouring the bill the Bills Payable Account is debited with the amou
of the settlement and the credit is entered in the Bank Account.

(*c*) *If the Bill is Dishonoured*

John White is unable to meet the bill on maturity so dishonouring the bi
Charges of £2 are incurred.

JOURNAL

Bills Payable	**Dr.** £100	
Charges	2	
To Robert Black		£102

Being bill drawn by Robert Black at three months dishonoured. Charges
incurred £2.

LEDGER

Dr.   *Bills Payable Account*   **Cr.**

Robert Black | £100 ‖ Balance | £100

Robert Black Account

                                          Bills Payable | £100
                                          Charges | 2

Charges Account

Robert Black | £2 ‖ |

When a bill is dishonoured the amount of the bill is transferred from the Bills Payable Account to the Creditor's Account thus establishing the position as it was prior to the bill being accepted. The charges arising from the dishonour of the bill are normally the responsibility of the party dishonouring the bill.

(d) If the Bill is Renewed

John White accepts a bill drawn by Robert Black for £105 in renewal of his bill payable which was currently due for payment. Interest charges amount to £5.

JOURNAL

            Bills Payable   **Dr.**   £100
            Interest   5
                To Robert Black   £105
Being bill now due to be met replaced by a new bill. Interest charges amount to £5.

            Robert Black   **Dr.**   £105
                To Bills Payable   £105
Being acceptance of bill drawn by Robert Black.

Dr.   *Bills Payable Account*   **Cr.**

Robert Black | £100 ‖ Balance | £100

                              ‖ Robert Black | £105

Robert Black Account

Bills Payable | £105 ‖ Bills Payable | £100
                              ‖ Interest | 5

                        | £105 ‖ | £105

Interest Account

Robert Black | £5 ‖ |

When a bill is renewed the former bill has to be cancelled by transferring the amount of the bill from the Bills Payable Account to the Creditor's Account before recording the entries for the replacement bill.

(e) *Discounting or Endorsing the Bill*

If the bill is discounted or endorsed by Robert Black no entries are required in the books of John White.

6.62 ENTRIES IN THE BOOKS OF THE DRAWER (ROBERT BLACK) TO WHOM IT IS A BILL RECEIVABLE

(a) *On Acceptance of the Bill*

Robert Black receives John White's acceptance of the bill at three months for £100 being the debt due by John White.

JOURNAL

Bills Receivable	**Dr.** £100	
To John White		£100

Being acceptance of bill by John White at three months.

LEDGER

Dr.   *Bills Receivable Account*   **Cr.**

John White | £100 ‖ |

John White Account

Balance | £100 ‖ Bills Receivable | £100

On receipt of John White's acceptance of the bill Robert Black is required to transfer the amount of the bill from John White's Account to a Bills Receivable Account thus reducing debtors and increasing bills receivable.

(b) *If the Bill is Discounted*

The bill accepted by John White is discounted at the bank. Bill discount charges amount to £3.

JOURNAL

Bank	**Dr.** £97	
Bill Discount	3	
To Bills Receivable		£100

Being bill accepted by John White discounted at Bank. Discount Charges amount to £3.

LEDGER

Dr.	Bills Receivable Account			Cr.
Balance	£100	Bank		£97
		Bill Discount		3
	———			———
	£100			£100

Bank Account

Bills Receivable	£97	

Bill Discount Account

Bills Receivable	£3	

When a bill is discounted the proceeds and any bill discount charges are credited to the Bills Receivable Account. The latter account, assuming there is only one bill in existence, will be closed since the bill of exchange will be held by the bank and not by Robert Black.

(c) If the Bill is Endorsed

Robert Black endorsed the bill accepted by John White to Tom Green, to whom he owed £100.

JOURNAL

Tom Green   **Dr.**   £100
   To Bills Receivable   £100
Being bill accepted by John White endorsed to Tom Green.

LEDGER

Dr.	Tom Green Account			Cr.
Bills Receivable	£100	Balance		£100

Bills Receivable Account

Balance	£100	Tom Green		£100

When a bill is endorsed the amount of the bill is transferred from the Bills Receivable Account to the account of the endorsee.

(d) On Honouring the Bill at Maturity

John White honours the bill at maturity.

JOURNAL

Bank	**Dr.** £100	
To Bills Receivable		£100

Being settlement of bill by John White.

LEDGER

Dr.   *Bills Receivable Account*   **Cr.**

Balance	£100	Bank	£100

Bank Account

Bills Receivable	£100

When the bill is met at maturity the Bills Receivable Account is credited with the proceeds of the bill.

(e) *If the Bill is Dishonoured*

John White failed to meet the bill on maturity. The charges incurred by the dishonour of the bill amount to £2 and were paid by Black.

JOURNAL

John White	**Dr.** £102	
To Bills Receivable		£100
Bank (Payment of charges)		2

Being bill dishonoured by John White. Charges amount to £2.

LEDGER

Dr.   *John White Account*   **Cr.**

Bills Receivable	£100	
Bank	2	

Bills Receivable Account

Balance	£100	John White	£100

Bank Account

	John White (charges)	£2

As John White has failed to honour the bill accepted by him, the amount of the bill is credited to the Bills Receivable Account and debited to White's Account. Also the charges paid by Black due to the dishonour of the bill by White are charged to White's Account.

(*f*) *If the Bill is Dishonoured and has Previously been Discounted*

John White dishonours the bill when presented for payment. The bill had been previously discounted by Robert Black. The charges incurred due to the dishonour of the bill amount to £2.

JOURNAL

John White   **Dr.** £102
     To Bank   £102

Being bill dishonoured by John White. Charges amount to £2.

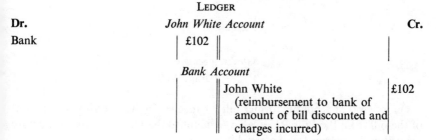

LEDGER

Dr.	*John White Account*	**Cr.**
Bank	£102	

Bank Account

	John White	£102
	(reimbursement to bank of	
	amount of bill discounted and	
	charges incurred)	

No entry is required in the Bills Receivable Account if the bill dishonoured has been previously discounted. Robert Black has to repay the bank the amount of the bill plus any charges and debit the total amount of this reimbursement to John White's Account.

(*g*) *If the Bill is Renewed*

John White's original acceptance for £100 has been renewed for a further period of three months. Interest charges amount to £5 and are to be added in the new bill.

JOURNAL

John White   **Dr.**   £100
     To Bills Receivable   £100

Being cancellation of bill accepted by John White, now renewed for a further period of three months.

John White   **Dr.**   £5
     To Interest   £5

Being interest charges on renewal of bill.

Bills Receivable   **Dr.**   £105
     To John White   £105

Being new bill accepted by John White for three months.

LEDGER

Dr.		John White Account		Cr.
Bills Receivable	£100	Bills Receivable		£105
Interest	5			
	£105			£105

		Bills Receivable Account		
Balance	£100	John White		£100
John White	£105			

		Interest Account		
		John White		£5

On renewal of a bill the former bill is cancelled by transferring the amount of the bill from the Bills Receivable Account to the Debtor's Account before recording the entries for the new bill.

If the original bill had been discounted by Robert Black then the Bank Account would have been credited with £100 and not Bills Receivable Account as shown in the first journal entry.

This example illustrates how the Bills of Exchange are recorded in each party's books.

Question

You are required to record in the Cash Book and Ledger of Murray and Band the following information.

Murray was indebted to Band on 31 March Year 2 for a sum of £600 for goods supplied to him. It was agreed that Band would draw three Bills of Exchange on Murray. The Bills were accepted by Murray on 1 April Year 2.

Bill for £300 at one month
Bill for £200 at two months
Bill for £100 at three months.

The second Bill was discounted on 3 April Year 2 by Band at 6%. The first and second Bills were met at maturity but the third Bill was dishonoured on presentation. The charges amounted to £1 and were paid by Band.

Suggested Solution:

IN THE BOOKS OF MURRAY

Dr.   CASH BOOK (Extract)   **Cr.**

			Year 2		
			May	4	Bills Payable	£300
			June	4	Bills Payable	200

Band Account

Year 2			Year 2			
Apr.	1	Bills Payable	£300	Mar. 31	Balance	£600
Apr.	1	Bills Payable	200	July	4	Bills Payable	100
Apr.	1	Bills Payable	100			Charges	1
July	4	Balance	101				
			£701			£701
				July	5	Balance	£101

Bills Payable Account

Year 2				Year 2			
May	4	Cash	£300	Apr.	1	Band	£300
June	4	Cash	200	Apr.	1	Band	200
July	4	Band	100	Apr.	1	Band	100
			£600				£600

Charges Account

Year 2				
July	4	Band	£1	

IN THE BOOKS OF BAND

Dr.   CASH BOOK (Extract)   **Cr.**

Year 2				Year 2			
Apr.	3	Bills Receivable	£198	July	4	Murray	£1
May	4	Bills Receivable	300				

Murray Account

Year 2				Year 2			
Mar. 31		Balance	£600	Apr.	1	Bills Receivable	£300
July	4	Bills Receivable	100	Apr.	1	Bills Receivable	200
		Cash	1	Apr.	1	Bills Receivable	100
				July	4	Balance	101
			£701				£701
July	5	Balance	£101				

Dr.   *Bills Receivable Account*   **Cr.**

Year 2			Year 2		
Apr. 1	Murray	£300	Apr. 3	Cash	£198
Apr. 1	Murray	200		Bill Discount	2
Apr. 1	Murray	100	May 4	Cash	300
			July 4	Murray	100
		£600			£600

Bill Discount Account

Year 2		
Apr. 3	Bills Receivable	£2

Examination Questions

Question 1

On 1 January Year 5, Black received from White his acceptance for three months for £1,000 for goods supplied on that date. He immediately discounted the Bill with his Bankers for £990. White dishonoured the Bill on the due date. Show the ledger entries to record the above in the books of Black.

Question 2

On 1 July Year 4, R. Johnson drew an accommodation bill on T. Bach for £150 at four months. The latter accepted the bill and Johnson discounted it on the same date at 6% per annum, the proceeds being shared equally. The bill was met in due course by Bach, who at the same time received the money due from Johnson. Show the transactions as they would appear in Bach's Cash Book and Ledger.

Question 3

From the following information you are required to write up the relevant ledger accounts in the books of Smith and Jones, indicating clearly with whose ledger you are dealing in each part of your answer.

(a) On 1 January Year 7, Smith sold goods on credit to Jones for £1,000 and to Black for £750. On the same day, Smith purchased goods from White for £1,200.

(b) Jones accepted a three months bill of exchange and Black one at six months on 1 February Year 7, both in full settlement of their accounts.

(c) Smith discounted Black's bill immediately at 5% per annum and endorsed the bill from Jones to White sending it to him with a cheque for £200.

(d) White discounted Jones' bill on 1 March Year 7 at 5% per annum. Subsequently when Jones' bill was presented for payment it was dishonoured.

(Discounting charges are to be calculated in months. It is important that all relevant dates should be inserted in the ledger accounts.)

Workings to nearest £.

(C. of S.)

Question 4

On 1 May Year 6, Angus and Blair draw on each other for £2,000 at six months. Both Bills are discounted at 5%. At maturity Angus meets his Bill, but Blair's Bill is dishonoured and taken up by Angus. Blair now remits to Angus £1,000 in cash and gives two Bills at three and six months of equal amount for the balance plus interest at 5% (£506·25 and £512·50) in settlement. The first of these is met but the second is dishonoured (charges £1). Blair is now bankrupt and his Estate pays, on 1 June Year 7, a first and final dividend of £0·50 in the £. Record the entries in the books of both Angus and Blair.

Question 5

Show the following accounts in the books of H. Bell:

(a) R. Mather
(b) T. Lyall
(c) Bills Receivable
(d) Bank

Record the undernoted information in these Accounts:

On 1 January Year 9, the books of H. Bell showed £200 due to T. Lyall and £400 due to R. Mather.

On 3 January Lyall accepted two Bills of Exchange to cover the amount due—one for £150, tenure one month; and one for £50, tenure two months.

The first of these Bell endorsed to Mather on 4 January, paying the balance due by cheque. The second he discounted on 5 January less £1 Bill discount. On the first Bill falling due Lyall was unable to meet it and Bell had to settle with Mather. On that date he renewed the Bill for another month with the addition of £5 for expenses and interest.

On the second Bill falling due Bell had to settle with the Bank, Lyall being unable to meet it. When the renewed Bill became due Lyall paid the amount due by cheque but was unable to pay the balance due by him. Ultimately he paid £0·50 in the £, the balance being irrecoverable.

7 Self-Balancing Ledgers and Control Accounts

7.1 THE NECESSITY FOR SELF-BALANCING LEDGERS AND CONTROL ACCOUNTS

If one has only had experience of working through examination problems, it may appear that any form of control over the accuracy of the posting of accounting entries is not of great importance, since it is quite a simple matter to check through the postings if an error is revealed in the Trial Balance and discover the difference. In practice, the discovery of posting errors may take a considerable time if the number of postings are numerous. In some businesses there are over ten thousand accounts in the sales ledger alone with perhaps an average of twenty entries in each account. If errors occur in an accounting system of that size one can well imagine how long it could take to find and rectify such mistakes without the aid of some control system. It is primarily for this reason that some system has to be introduced to assist in the locating of errors. The technique generally adopted to surmount this problem is to introduce self-balancing ledgers. Self-balancing ledgers are commonly found in the Purchases and Sales Ledgers where entries are numerous and posting errors most likely to occur. It must be appreciated that the system of self-balancing ledgers is introduced only to assist in the detection of arithmetical errors in the double entry system. It will not reveal compensating errors, errors in books of original entry, and postings to wrong accounts which have taken place in the recording of the transactions. In this sense it is similar to a Trial Balance. This system can be employed both for hand written and machine accounting records.

7.2 ADVANTAGES OF SELF-BALANCING LEDGERS

1. A simple yet effective control can be kept on the arithmetical accuracy of the postings from the books of original entry to the ledger.
2. It is invaluable under a system of mechanized accounting since work may be delegated by the office manager to several accounting machine

operators and a control maintained over the work at each stage of posting.

3. It may serve as a check on the honesty of the accounting staff if used as a part of an internal check system.

4. Total balances for debtors and creditors can be quickly ascertained with reference to the Total or Control Accounts. This is useful in the preparation of monthly or quarterly financial statements, pending the extraction of complete lists of debtors and creditors.

7.3 CONSTRUCTION OF A PURCHASES LEDGER TOTAL ACCOUNT

To make the Purchases Ledger self-balancing a Total Account is opened at the end of the ledger into which are posted in summarized form all the detailed entries in the ledger to which it refers. The amounts appearing in the Total Account are not summarized from the ledger accounts but are taken from the books of original entry from which the detailed postings were entered. The entries in the Total Account appear on the opposite side from the corresponding detailed entries in the individual ledger accounts. In this way a trial balance can be extracted from the Purchase Ledger. The total of the individual balances appearing in the ledger would form a credit balance in the trial balance and the balance of the Total Account would be a debit balance. The balance on the Total Account should agree with the list of balances extracted from the ledger. Should the balances not be in agreement it would indicate that either an error has been made in the construction of the Total Account or that mistakes have arisen in the postings from the books of original entry to the ledger or in the additions of these books.

To illustrate the function of a Total Account the following example is shown. The number of entries has been kept to a minimum for simplicity.

The following accounts appear in the Purchases Ledger of W. Smith:

Dr.			*J. Todd Account*			Cr.
Jan. 26	Cash	£35	Jan. 1	Balance		£300
	Discount	1	Jan. 5	Goods		20
Jan. 31	Balance	284				
		£320				£320
			Feb. 1	Balance		£284

Dr.   *L. Brown Account*   **Cr.**

Jan. 30	Returns	£5	Jan. 1	Balance	£95
	Cash	40	Jan. 16	Goods	35
Jan. 31	Balance	85			
		£130			£130
			Feb. 1	Balance	£85

W. Green Account

| Jan. 1 | Balance | £5 | Jan. 10 | Cash | £5 |

The construction of the Purchases Ledger Total Account is shown in Figure 3. By examining the account and comparing the closing balance with the list of balances extracted from the ledger both are seen to agree proving that correct arithmetical postings have been made from the books of original entry to the ledger thus satisfying the main objective of self-balancing ledgers. To facilitate the compilation of a Total Account special columns are allocated in the Cash Book for amounts posted to the Purchases Ledger. In this way it is possible to take totals from the Cash Book and transfer them to the Total Account without further analysis.

7.4   CONSTRUCTION OF A SALES LEDGER TOTAL ACCOUNT

To make the Sales Ledger self-balancing a Total Account is opened at the end of the Sales Ledger to which are transferred in summarized form from the books of original entry all amounts which have been posted in detail to the ledger accounts. The amounts in the Total Account will, of course, appear on the opposite sides from the corresponding detailed entries in the individual ledger accounts. This ensures that a trial balance can be extracted from the ledger at the balancing date. The balance on the Total Account should always be in agreement with the total balances shown from the ledger. This proof may be carried out at fixed intervals during the firm's financial year so that if any disagreement between the balances occurs it is not so difficult a task to trace the errors say on a monthly basis compared with checking through twelve months' entries. The Sales Ledger Total Account is constructed in a similar way to the Purchases Ledger Total Account and is illustrated in the following example. Again the entries have been limited to simplify the problem.

Figure 3. Construction of Purchases Ledger Total Account

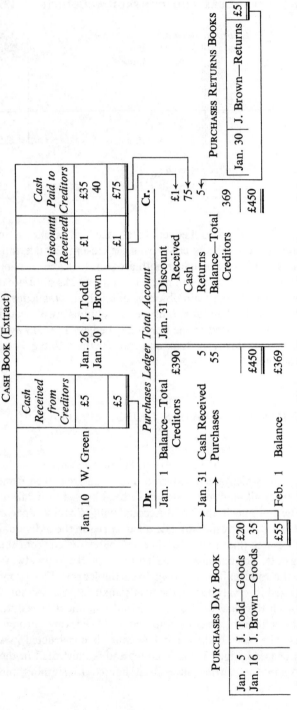

CASH BOOK (Extract)

		Cash Received from Creditors			Discount Received	Cash Paid to Creditors
Jan. 10	W. Green	£5	Jan. 26	J. Todd	£1	£35
			Jan. 30	J. Brown		40
		£5			£1	£75

Purchases Ledger Total Account

Dr.				Cr.	
Jan. 1	Balance—Total Creditors	£390	Jan. 31	Discount Received	£1
Jan. 31	Cash Received	5		Cash	75
	Purchases	55		Returns	5
				Balance—Total Creditors	369
		£450			£450
Feb. 1	Balance	£369			

PURCHASES DAY BOOK

Jan. 5	J. Todd—Goods	£20
Jan. 16	J. Brown—Goods	35
		£55

PURCHASES RETURNS BOOKS

Jan. 30	J. Brown—Returns	£5

Notes: 1. The Balance as at 1 Jan. will be the Balance brought down from the previous period.
2. The closing Balance as at 31 Jan. should equal the Balances per Purchases Ledger as shown below.

TRIAL BALANCE OF PURCHASES LEDGER

J. Todd	£284	
J. Brown	85	
Purchases Ledger Total Account		£369
	£369	£369

The following accounts appear in the Sales Ledger of W. Smith:

Dr. *J. Smith Account* **Cr.**

Jan. 1	Balance	£100	Jan. 25	Cash	£75
Jan. 17	Goods	50		Discount	5
			Jan. 31	Balance	70
		£150			£150
Feb. 1	Balance	£70			

R. Brown Account

Jan. 1	Balance	£20	Jan. 31	Cash	£50
Jan. 21	Goods	60		Returns	10
				Balance	20
		£80			£80
Feb. 1	Balance	£20			

A. Field Account

Jan. 1	Balance	£16	Jan. 31	Bad Debt	£16

T. Bell Account

Jan. 26	Cash	£10	Jan. 1	Balance	£10

The construction of the Sales Ledger Total Account is shown in Figure 4. From the illustration it will be noticed that the closing balance of £90 in the Total Account is in agreement with the list of balances extracted from the ledger. Again separate columns are reserved in the Cash Book for those amounts posted to the Sales Ledger. This facilitates the compilation of the Total Account. As well as taking the relevant totals from the Cash Book and Day Books to the Total Account it is also necessary to scrutinize the Journal to ascertain if any items refer to the Sales Ledger. In this illustration an amount was written off as a bad debt in the Sales Ledger so this sum will require to be shown in the Total Account at the balancing date.

7.5 PURCHASES AND SALES LEDGER CONTROL ACCOUNTS

When self-balancing ledgers are introduced into an accounting system for the Sales and Purchases Ledgers it is usual to include Purchases and Sales Ledger

FIGURE 4. Construction of Sales Ledger Total Account

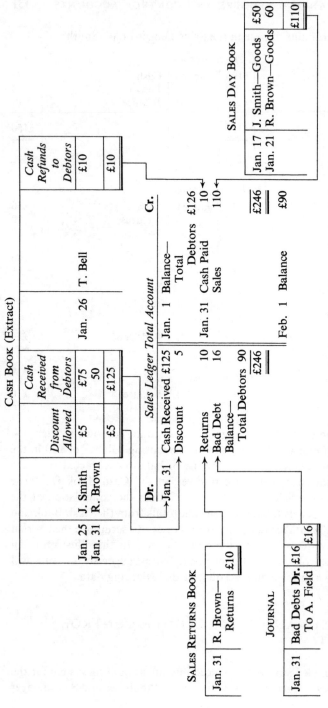

Notes: 1. The Balance as at 1 Jan. will be the Balance brought down from the previous period.
2. The closing Balance as at 31 Jan. should equal the Balances per Sales Ledger as shown below.

Control Accounts in the Impersonal Ledger. Those accounts would be compiled in the same way as Total Accounts in the Purchases and Sales Ledger, the only difference being that the amounts are shown on the reverse sides of the Accounts.

If Control Accounts were kept in the Impersonal Ledger for the two examples considered earlier in the chapter, they would appear as follows:

IMPERSONAL LEDGER

Dr. *Purchases Ledger Control Account* **Cr.**

			£				£
Jan. 31	Returns		5	Jan. 1	Balance		390
	Cash		75	Jan. 31	Purchases		55
	Discount		1		Cash Received		5
	Balance		369				
			£450				£450
				Feb. 1	Balance		£369

Sales Ledger Control Account

			£				£
Jan. 1	Balance		126	Jan. 31	Cash		125
Jan. 31	Sales		110		Discount		5
	Cash Paid		10		Returns		10
					Bad Debt		16
					Balance		90
			£246				£246
Feb. 1	Balance		£90				

By introducing these accounts into the Impersonal Ledger a measure of control can be exercised over the personnel responsible for the Purchases and Sales Ledgers. The Accountant or Office Manager can compare the balances brought out in the Control Accounts with those shown in the Total Accounts. Furthermore, by including Control Accounts in the Impersonal Ledger, this ledger becomes in itself self-balancing and a Trial Balance may be extracted without reference to the Purchases and Sales Ledger. For this purpose the Cash Book balances would require to be included with the balances in the Impersonal Ledger. In the Trial Balance the balances shown on the Purchases and Sales Ledger Control Accounts would be entered representing the total creditors and debtors at the balancing date.

7.6   SUB-DIVISION OF PURCHASES AND SALES LEDGERS

Due to the large number of accounts recorded in the Purchases and Sales Ledgers it may be necessary to sub-divide the ledgers. This sub-division may take place on an alphabetical basis such as:

Purchases Ledger	A–L and M–Z
Sales Ledger	A–G, H–O, and P–Z

When this arises separate Total Accounts are prepared for each division of the ledger and corresponding Control Accounts are opened in the Impersonal Ledger. So that the relevant totals can be recorded in the Total Accounts it is necessary to sub-divide the books of original entry in order that totals for each division of the ledger may be shown separately in these books. An illustration of this is shown in Figure 5.

Question

The following figures are taken from the books of Adam Smith & Co., at 31 December Year 8:

Sales Ledger balances at 1 Dec. Year 8	£4,873
Purchases Ledger balances at 1 Dec. Year 8	2,400
Sales, *less* Returns	22,910
Purchases, *less* Returns	18,550
Cash received from debtors	21,002
Cash paid to creditors	18,190
Bill of Exchange accepted by debtor	250
Discounts allowed	410
Discounts received	351
Bad Debts written off	15
Interest charged by creditor on overdue account	25
Accounts settled by transfer from one ledger to the other	47

Prepare Control Accounts to record the above information for the month ended 31 December Year 8.

FIGURE 5

PURCHASES DAY BOOK

Date	Details	Folio	Total	Purchases Ledger	
				A–L	M–Z

CASH BOOK (Credit Side)

Date	Details	Folio	Discount		Total	Purchases Ledger	
			A–L	M–Z		A–L	M–Z

Notes: 1. The Purchases Returns Book would be ruled in a similar form.
2. The Columns would be reserved on the Debit Side of the Cash Book for Cash Received from Creditors.

SALES DAY BOOK

Date	Details	Folio	Total	Sales Ledgers		
				A–G	H–O	P–Z

CASH BOOK (Debit Side)

Date	Details	Folio	Discount			Total	Sales Ledger	
			A–G	H–O	P–Z		A–G	H–O P–Z

Notes: 1. The Sales Returns Book would be ruled in a similar form.
2. Three columns would be reserved on the credit side of the Cash Book for Cash Refunds to Debtors.

Suggested Solution:

Dr.		Sales Ledger Control Account			Cr.
Year 8			Year 8		
Dec. 1	Balance	£4,873	Dec. 31	Cash	£21,002
Dec. 31	Sales	22,910		Discount allowed	410
				Bill Receivable	250
				Contra (Purchase Ledger)	47
				Bad Debts	15
				Balance	6,059
		£27,783			£27,783

Dr.		Purchases Ledger Control Account			Cr.
Year 8			Year 8		
Dec. 31	Cash	£18,190	Dec. 1	Balance	£2,400
	Discount received	351	Dec. 31	Purchases	18,550
	Contra (Sales Ledger)	47		Interest	25
	Balance	2,387			
		£20,975			£20,975

Notes: 1. It must always be remembered that items appear on the same side in the Control Account as they do in the individual ledger accounts. This position is reversed, of course, when preparing Total Accounts.

2. When a question states that a Control Account is to be prepared it should be shown on the above form. The distinction between a Control Account and a Total Account must always be appreciated.

Examination Questions

Question 1

(a) State the advantages to be expected from the introduction of sales and purchases ledger control accounts in a double entry book-keeping system.

(b) Prepare a specimen sales ledger control account for one month during which sales are made, allowances are given for returns, cash is received, discount is allowed, and a bad debt is written off.

(C.A.)

Question 2

From the following details you are required to prepare Purchases and Sales Ledger Control Accounts for the month of July Year 7.

July 1		
Purchases Ledger Balances		£2,940
Sales Ledger Balances		4,936
Totals for month ending 31 July:		
Purchases Day Book		5,201
Purchases Returns Book		612
Sales Day Book		7,315
Sales Returns Book		30
Cheques paid to Creditors		5,110
Cheques Received from Debtors		6,985
Discount Received		40
Discount Allowed		82
Bad Debts written off		15
Debtor's Cheque dishonoured		22
Balances on the Sales Ledger set off against credit balances in the Purchases Ledger		43

Question 3

The trial balance of Oxleigh & Co. fails to agree. You are convinced that the error lies somewhere in the debtors or creditors ledgers, and in consequence you decide to prepare Control Accounts for those ledgers in order to locate the error. From the following information you are requested to prepare those Control Accounts and to ascertain the amount of the error, and where it may be found.

Purchases ledger balances brought forward	£6,267
Purchases for year	81,062
Returns inwards	2,416
Cheques paid to suppliers	75,261
Discounts allowed	3,016
Returns outwards	792
Cash and cheques received from customers	94,617
Discounts received	1,023
Sales ledger balances brought forward	11,168
Sales to customers for year	102,413
Balances in sales ledger set off against balances in purchases ledger	719
Bad Debts written off	217
Cheques dishonoured	98

The detailed balances taken from the personal ledgers were—Creditors £9,534; Debtors £12,616.

(L. Ch. of C.)

Question 4

Discuss the functions served by Debtors and Creditors Control Accounts.
(C.I.S.)

Question 5

Prepare a creditors' ledger control account and a debtors' ledger control
account for April Year 7, from the following information:

At 1 April Year 7.

Creditors' ledger balances	£3,282
Debtors' ledger balances	8,884
Provision for bad debts	177

Totals for April Year 7.

Sales invoices sent	£10,322
Purchases invoices received	9,389
Returns outward	528
Returns inward	280
Allowances by suppliers	89
Allowances to customers	23
Bills receivable accepted	392
Bad debts written off	254
Receipts for cash sales	987
Bad debts previously written off, now recovered	18
Bills receivable dishonoured	33
Interest charged on customer's overdue account	3
Cash paid to suppliers	9,325
Cash received from customers	9,873
Cash discount allowed	89
Cash discount received	183
Dishonoured cheque included in total cash received from customers (above)	98
Cash discount which had been allowed on dishonoured cheque (above)	2
Payments to supplier for cash purchases	1,231

At 30 April Year 7.

Contra item: B. Jones is both a customer and a supplier. In the purchases ledger he has a balance of £22 and in the sales ledger a balance
of £56. A net balance is to be shown.

The account of A. Brown (a customer) has a credit balance of	£27
Provision for bad debts	250

Question 6

From the following particulars you are required to show the sales ledger and purchases ledger control accounts as they would appear in the nominal ledger of Stewart & Co. for the year ended 31 December Year 2:

(a) The balances on the control accounts at 1 January Year 2 were:

Sales Ledger	£4,320
Purchases Ledger	2,198

(b) The following is an abstract of the cash book for the year:

Dr.					Cr.
Cash on hand, 1 Jan.			Purchases Ledger	£20,939	
Year 2		£346	*Less:* Discount	640	
					£20,299
Sales Ledger	£31,508		Bank Lodged		34,066
Less: Discount	473				
		31,035	Wages		11,482
Cash Sales		4,821	Expenses		1,337
Bank drawn		29,921	Sales Ledger		243
Bills discounted		1,216	Miscellaneous		2,001
Miscellaneous		2,379	Cash on hand,		
			31 Dec. Year 2		290
		£69,718			£69,718

(c) Day book totals for the year are:

Purchases		*Sales*	
Goods	£19,713	Goods	£33,382
General Expenses	1,465	Miscellaneous	494
Miscellaneous	333		
	£21,511		£33,876

Returns Outwards		*Returns Inward*	
Goods	£521	Goods	£743
Miscellaneous	36	Miscellaneous	72
	£557		£815

(d) The bills receivable book shows that bills totalling £1,350 were received during the year. These were all in respect of sales ledger accounts and none has been dishonoured.

The following information was ascertained after the figures from the books of original entry as above had been posted to the nominal ledger. Assume that any adjustments necessary have been made by journal entry:

(i) On the credit side of the cash book the wages column has been over-summed and the sales ledger column under-summed, both by £10.

(ii) Goods amounting to £61 taken by the owner of the business for his own use have been included in the sales day book. These goods were in fact paid for by him in cash at the time and are included in cash sales.

(iii) The total and general expenses columns of the purchase day book have both been under-summed by £99.

(iv) A bad debt of £105, written off in the year to 31 December Year 1, has been recovered to the extent of £47 and this sum is included in the cash sales column of the cash book.

(v) Goods amounting to £153, sent to a customer on a sale or return basis on 22 December Year 2, were entered in the sales day book. Acceptance of the goods had not been intimated by 31 December Year 2, and they were included at their cost price of £88 in stock on hand at that date.

You are not required to draft the actual journal entries.

(C.A.)

8 Manufacturing Accounts

8.1 INTRODUCTION

One of the principal functions of accounting is providing information for management. To achieve this, care and consideration must be given to ensure that financial data are presented to management in a purposeful manner to ensure accurate assessment of past results and to aid future policy making. This applies not only to the final accounts but to all financial statements. In the final form, accounts are divided into two sections referred to as the Trading Account and the Profit and Loss Account. This layout is usually adequate in a non-manufacturing concern which is only trading in finished goods, but not all businesses are in that category since many are engaged in the manufacture of goods and the information disclosed by a Trading Account would not be sufficient to meet the requirements of management. To overcome this problem and to present the accounts in greater detail, a Manufacturing Account is preferred which is designed to reveal the factory cost of the goods produced. This account is prepared in addition to the Trading Account, and the factory cost of goods produced, calculated in the Manufacturing Account, is transferred to the Trading Account and replaces the usual purchases figure. Thereafter the gross profit is calculated in the usual manner.

8.2 MANUFACTURING COSTS

Manufacturing Accounts cannot always be drafted to a standard pattern due to the complexity of manufacturing operations. Each manufacturing concern must design a form of account best suited to its own requirements. It may be that in certain businesses involved in the manufacture of several products there is a necessity to prepare a Manufacturing Account for each product in order to give product costs as well as total factory cost of goods produced. Although standardization is not always possible in the design the following elements of cost are usually shown in the Manufacturing Account:

1. Prime Cost.
2. Factory Cost.
3. Factory Cost of Finished Goods.

8.21 PRIME COST

Although different opinions are held as to the meaning of this term and what items should be included in this section of the Manufacturing Account it is better at least for the student at this stage to be familiar with the usually accepted items making up this element of cost. Items to be included are:

Opening Stock of Raw Materials
Raw Materials Purchased (materials that enter into and become a part of the finished product)
    Less: Closing Stock of Raw Materials
Carriage on Raw Materials
Direct Wages (wages paid which can be identified with manufacture)

The value of rejected materials or by-products will be credited to the cost of raw materials purchased or deleted from the prime cost.

8.22 FACTORY COST

Factory Cost is Prime Cost (i.e. direct labour, material, and expenses) plus all indirect expenses of manufacture, which cannot be classified as direct material, direct labour, or direct expenses. The items of indirect expenditure include:

Rent and Rates of Factory
Factory Heat, Light, and Power
Plant and Machinery repairs and maintenance
Depreciation of plant and machinery used in the factory
Indirect Wages (works manager's salary, store keeping wages, etc.)

To prepare detailed Manufacturing, Trading, and Profit and Loss Accounts it is necessary to allocate costs of a similar nature between factory, warehouse, and office. For example, a business may pay a rent of £10,000 per annum for a building but it would be incorrect to charge the whole amount to the cost of manufacturing the goods if part of the rented premises is used for a dispatch warehouse and an office block. Obviously an apportionment of the total rent charge would require to be made, possibly on the basis of floor space used, and a charge made on that basis to the factory cost, selling and distribution cost, and administrative cost.

8.23 FACTORY COST OF FINISHED GOODS

When the total factory cost has been established an adjustment is made on this amount in respect of Work-in-progress as follows:

Factory Cost

> *Add:* Work-in-Progress at beginning of period
> *Less:* Work-in-Progress at end of period

Work-in-Progress is the value of incomplete work in the factory and is usually computed on the following basis:

> The cost of materials and production labour plus the proportion of indirect expenses chargeable to the work up to its present stage of manufacture.

8.24 STOCK OF RAW MATERIALS AND FINISHED GOODS

Care has to be taken in dealing with stocks of raw materials and finished goods. Stocks of raw materials are shown in the Manufacturing Account in the prime cost section while stocks of finished goods are recorded in the Trading Account in the usual way. It is important to ensure that stocks are valued on a consistent basis and that no element of profit is included in the valuation. It will be appreciated from the study of accounting so far that an incorrect valuation of stock can have a serious effect on the amount of trading profit or loss of a business.

Question

From the following information supplied by the Modern Machine Manu-facturing Company you are required to prepare a Manufacturing, Trading, and Profit and Loss Account for the year ended 31 December Year 9.

Stocks 1 Jan. Year 9	
Raw Materials	£3,000
Work-in-Progress	1,000
Finished Goods	4,500
Stocks 31 Dec. Year 9	
Raw Materials	1,500
Work-in-Progress	2,500
Finished Goods	3,600
Carriage on Raw Materials	2,750
Sales	80,000
Factory Rent and Rates	250
Factory Heat, Light, and Power	1,200
Depreciation on Factory Plant	2,800
Travellers' Salaries	5,500
Advertising	1,250
Office Rent and Rates	300
Office Salaries	3,500
Carriage Outwards	700
Purchases of Raw Materials	50,000
Direct Wages	7,000
Plant Repairs	210
Factory Expenses	75

Suggested Solution:

MODERN MACHINE MANUFACTURING COMPANY

Manufacturing Account for Year ended 31 December Year 9

Raw Materials pur- chased	£50,000		Factory Cost of Finished Goods		£64,285
Add: Stock of Raw Materials 1 Jan. Year 9	3,000				
	53,000				
Less: Stock of Raw Materials 31 Dec. Year 9	1,500				
	51,500				
Carriage on raw Materials	2,750				
		54,250			
Direct Wages		7,000			
Prime Cost		61,250			
Factory Rent and Rates	250				
Factory Heat, Light, and Power	1,200				
Plant Repairs	210				
Factory Expenses	75				
Depreciation on Fac- tory Plant	2,800	4,535			
Factory Cost		65,785			
Adjustment for Work in Progress: As at 1 Jan. As at 31 Dec.	1,000 2,500				
		1,500			
		£64,285			£64,285

Trading Account for Year ended 31 December Year 9

Factory Cost of			Sales		£80,000
Finished Goods	£64,285				
Add: Stock of					
finished goods					
at 1 Jan.	4,500				
	——				
	68,785				
Less: Stock of finished					
goods at 31 Dec.	3,600				
	——	65,185			
Gross Profit for Year		14,815			
		——			——
		£80,000			£80,000

Profit and Loss Account for Year ended 31 December Year 9

Administration			Gross Profit	14,815
Expenses				
Office Salaries	£3,500			
Office Rent and Rates	300			
	——	3,800		
Selling Expenses				
Travellers' Salaries	5,500			
Advertising	1,250			
Carriage Outwards	700			
	——	7,450		
Profit for Year		3,565		
		——		——
		£14,815		£14,815

Examination Questions

Question 1

The following balances were extracted from the books of Hill and Dale at 31 December Year 9.

Manufacturing Wages	£39,205	Factory Expenses	£3,090
Raw Material Consumed	92,310	Carriage Outwards	2,570
Work in Progress	6,176	Selling Expenses	6,230
Stock—Finished Goods	13,902	Office Expenses	3,005
Carriage Inwards	2,296	Discounts Received	1,112
Heating and Lighting	1,721	Discounts Allowed	2,132
Fuel and Power	7,293	Sales for Year	221,549
Rates and Insurances	2,510		

You are required to prepare the firm's Manufacturing Account for the year ended 31 December Year 9. Thereafter you are to prepare the Trading and Profit and Loss Account for the same period.

Further information:

(a) Depreciation is to be provided as follows:

Office Furniture and Fixtures	£1,250
Plant and Machinery	2,000

(b) Closing Stocks are:

Work in Progress	£8,000
Finished Goods	14,344

Question 2

From the following information you are required to prepare Manufacturing, Trading, and Profit and Loss Accounts:

Stock of Finished Goods 1 Jan.	£1,700
Stock of Raw Materials 1 Jan.	9,000
Work in Progress 1 Jan.	1,500
Purchases of Raw Materials	145,000
Sales of Finished Goods	405,000
Trade Discounts on Raw Materials	2,000
Discount Allowed	3,000
General Office Expenses	19,000
Office Salaries	21,000
Carriage Outwards	2,500
Factory Wages	157,000
Factory Expenses	10,000
Depreciation of Plant and Machinery	15,000
Depreciation of Factory Buildings	700
Depreciation of Office Buildings	200
Stock of Finished Goods 31 Dec.	13,000
Stock of Raw Materials 31 Dec.	7,000
Work in Progress 31 Dec.	2,800

Question 3

George Smith has been in business for a number of years as a manufacturer. The following balances have been extracted from his books on 31 December Year 8, and you are required to prepare from these balances and the additional information given in the question, a Manufacturing Account,

Trading Account, and Profit and Loss Account for the year ended 31 December.

Capital Account		£45,000
Office Equipment—Cost	£2,500	
Depreciation Provision		700
Factory Expenses	2,700	
Office Expenses	1,900	
Sales		90,000
Drawings	1,500	
Carriage Inwards	900	
Carriage Outwards	1,200	
Factory Buildings	10,000	
Purchases—Raw Materials	36,000	
Heat, Light and Power:		
Factory	1,800	
Office	200	
Stocks—Raw Materials	6,050	
Finished Goods	18,000	
Work in Progress	1,200	
Discount Allowed	1,400	
Cash at Bank	7,000	
Cash in Hand	50	
Plant and Machinery—Cost	15,000	
Depreciation		
Provision		5,000
Debtors	14,300	
Creditors		4,750
Factory Wages	18,400	
Office Salaries	6,800	
Rates and Insurance—Factory	800	
Office	150	
Bills Payable		2,400
	£147,850	£147,850

Additional Information

(a)

Stocks—Raw Materials	£7,800
Finished Goods	14,300
Work in Progress	1,100

(b) Depreciation has to be provided as follows:

Plant and Machinery	10% on cost
Office Equipment	5% on cost

(c) Office Salaries to be accrued £300

Rates to be prepaid—Factory	£50
Office	£30

(d) Bad Debts of £70 to be written off.

Question 4

George English is in business as a manufacturer. The following information is extracted from his books at 31 December Year 9:

Capital	£45,900
Buildings at cost	24,000
Machinery and Plant at Cost	23,000
Stocks at 1 Jan. Year 9:	
Raw Materials	3,000
Work in Progress	4,600
Finished Goods	3,600
Provision for Depreciation to 31 Dec. Year 9:	
Buildings	4,000
Machinery and Plant	10,000
Sales	92,000
Drawings	8,000
Salesmen's Salaries and Expenses	5,000
Bad Debts	50
Advertising Campaign	4,050
Heat and Light	500
Rates	600
Wages: Warehouse	2,000
Manufacturing	15,100
Printing and Stationery	2,100
Purchases: Raw Materials	21,200
Finished Goods	22,900
Carriage Inwards on Raw Materials	600
Administration Expenses	1,200
Motor Vehicle Expenses	1,300
Debtors	13,000
Trade Creditors	6,500
Cash at Bank and in Hand	3,000
Expenses in advance at 31 Dec. Year 9	1,900
Creditors for Expenses	2,300

Further Information: (a) It has been agreed that £1,000 of the cost of the advertising campaign is to be charged in Year 9.

(b) Depreciation is to be provided:

Machinery and Plant	£2,000
Buildings	1,000

(c) Stocks at 31 December Year 9 were valued as follows:

Raw Materials	£2,000
Work in Progress	4,500
Finished Goods	4,100

From the above information you are required to prepare Manufacturing, Trading, and Profit and Loss Accounts for Year 9 together with a Balance Sheet as at 31 December Year 9.

9 Incomplete Records

9.1 INTRODUCTION

Many small firms do not observe the principles of double entry accounting in the recording of business transactions. Lack of knowledge of accounts on the part of the owner or the failure to employ someone who is conversant with the principles of accounting are perhaps the main reasons for this situation. Many businessmen do not consider the accurate recording of business transactions an important factor in successful trading. This, of course, results in accounting entries being inadequately recorded and if records are kept they are usually in a most unorthodox form. Since variations in the methods of recording transactions occur so frequently it is quite impossible to illustrate all possible systems. The term used to embrace all systems which fall short of the conventional double entry system of accounting is 'Incomplete Records'. Students of accounting must be skilled in the preparation of final accounts from incomplete records as not only is this an important examination topic but examiners in accounting consider that solving problems of this type is a real test of a student's knowledge and appreciation of the principles of double entry accounting. Study of this subject will soon reveal that a sound understanding of the principles of double entry accounting is essential if one is to prepare accounts from incomplete records.

Systems of incomplete records may be broadly classified as follows:

(a) Single entry accounting system.
(b) Single entry accounting system with the introduction of a cash book.

9.2 SINGLE ENTRY ACCOUNTING SYSTEM

Single entry accounting is, as the title suggests, basically a system which only records one aspect of each transaction, viz. the personal aspect. Consequently the only necessary book required to be written up under this system is the ledger. No other books are kept.

For example if a credit purchase is made by T. Smith from W. Day for £100 on 1 December and paid on 15 December in cash, the entries for such a transaction would only be entered in the ledger.

IN THE LEDGER OF T. SMITH

Dr.	*W. Day Account*			**Cr.**
Dec. 15	Cash	£100	Dec. 1	Goods	£100

No other entries would be made. In other words only one entry would be recorded for each transaction. The corresponding entries in the Purchases Account and in the Cash Book would not be made.

It is apparent from such a system that the accounting information is not as comprehensive as in a system of double entry accounting. For example, it is not possible under this system to prepare Trading and Profit and Loss Accounts showing details of revenue expenditure and income since details of purchases, sales, and revenue expenditure are not kept; only debtors and creditors are known. Although a detailed statement of profit or loss cannot be prepared it is still possible to determine the profit or loss of a business for a trading period with reasonable accuracy. This is achieved by compiling a Balance Sheet or Statement of Affairs at the beginning and end of the trading period under review. The term 'Statement of Affairs' is one commonly used in the subject of incomplete records and may be defined as a list of assets and liabilities. The difference between the net assets or capital accounts at the beginning and end of the trading period will determine the overall profit or loss for that period. This is based on the formula that net assets or capital at the end of the period less net assets or capital at the beginning of the period = profit for the period. A profit arises where the net assets or capital at the end of the trading period exceed those at the beginning of the trading period. On the other hand if the net assets at the beginning of the trading period are in excess of those at the end of the period then a loss has taken place.

This formula can only be used to calculate the profit or loss if the owner of the business has not introduced or withdrawn any amounts from the business during the trading period. If such transactions have taken place then the formula has to be expanded to meet this change and becomes:

Net Assets or Capital at End of Period		£X
Add: Drawings for Period	£X	
Less: Capital Introduced during Period	X	X
		—
		X
Less: Net Assets or Capital at Beginning of Period		X
		—
Profit or Loss for Period		£X

Net Assets in this Formula are total Assets less Liabilities

9.21 PREPARATION OF STATEMENT OF AFFAIRS OR BALANCE SHEET

As the ledger is the only book of account maintained under a system of single entry accounting there will be only details of debtors and creditors recorded in the business records. All other amounts required for inclusion in the Balance Sheet will have to be calculated or estimated at the end of the trading period. The additional information required to produce a Statement of Affairs or Balance Sheet may be listed thus:

(a) Valuation of Fixed Assets.
(b) Valuation of Stock.
(c) List of Accrued and Unexpired Charges.
(d) Estimate of Cash and Bank Balances.
(e) Estimated drawings of owner.
(f) Amount of capital, if any, introduced by owner during year.

Those estimates and valuations have, in most cases, to be prepared by the owner of the business and supplied to his professional accountant so that a Balance Sheet or Statement of Affairs may be produced. Obviously, the accuracy of the Balance Sheet and the resulting computation of profit and loss, depend to a large extent on the precise information given by the owner of the business. This last statement has greater practical significance than theoretical but is made to illustrate the problems arising in practice on this subject.

This is a problem illustrating the application of the formula to calculate profit from a single entry system of accounting.

Question

The following information relates to A. Carr's business:

Assets and Liabilities at	1 Jan.	31 Dec.
Fixtures	£900	£810
Debtors	240	290
Stock	1,200	1,440
Creditors	400	550
Cash	38	12
Balance at Bank	780	230
Loan from B. Burton	300	100
Motor Vehicle		800

During the year A. Carr had sold private investments for £200 which he paid into the Business Account, and he had drawn out £10 weekly for private use.

You are required to prepare a Statement showing the amount of the Profit or Loss for the year and a Balance Sheet at 31 December.

Suggested Solution:

Calculation of Profit for the Year ended 31 December

Net Assets at 31 December

Fixtures			£810
Motor Vehicle			800
Debtors			290
Stock			1,440
Bank			230
Cash			12
			3,582
Less: Creditors	£550		
Loan—B. Burton	100		
		650	
			£2,932
Add: Drawings (52 × £10)			520
			3,452
Less: Capital introduced			
Proceeds of sale of private investment			200
			3,252
Less: Net Assets at 1 Jan. (Note 1)			2,458
Profit for Year			£794

Balance Sheet as at 31 December

Capital			Fixed Assets		
As at 1 Jan.	£2,458		Fixtures	£810	
Add: Profit for Year	794		Motor Vehicle	800	
Proceeds of Sale					£1,610
of Private Invest-			Current Assets		
ment	200		Stock	1,440	
			Debtors	290	
	3,452		Bank	230	
Less: Drawings	520		Cash	12	
		£2,932			1,972
Current Liabilities					
Creditors	550				
Loan—B. Burton	100				
		650			
		£3,582			£3,582

Working Notes

1. *Calculation of Net Assets of A. Carr at 1 January*

Fixtures		£900
Debtors		240
Stock		1,200
Bank		780
Cash		38
		£3,158
Less: Loan from B. Burton	£300	
Creditors	400	
		700
		£2,458

Notes to Students

1. The proceeds of Sale of private investment is treated as capital introduced since this investment was not a business asset but a private one.
2. Notice the use of the formula: (Net Assets at end + Drawings for period — Capital introduced during period) — net assets at beginning = Profit for trading period, in solving this problem.

This is a more difficult question illustrating the calculation of profit from single entry records.

Question

AH has a building and house-repair business. On 30 September Year 5, his balance sheet was:

			Cost	Depreciation	
Proprietor's Capital	£4,000	Plant	£1,102	292	£810
Loan Account	1,000	Motor Vehicles	700	120	580
Trade Creditors	340		1,802	412	1,390
		Work in Progress		3,600	
		Less: Deposits		460	
					3,140
		Stock			620
		Debtors			170
		Cash			20
	£5,340				£5,340

During the winter of Year 5, his wife, who acted as his bookkeeper, died, and since then the books of account have not been properly kept. At 30 September Year 8, AH is able to make the following estimate of his financial position:

Plant (at cost less depreciation)	£1,750
Motor vehicles (at cost less depreciation)	600
Work in progress	5,150
Deposits	710
Stock	1,455
Debtors	205
Cash	1,085
Trade Creditors	508

During the period since the last Balance Sheet, these additional events have occurred:

1. AH has withdrawn £15 in cash each week.
2. A cement-mixer, with a book value of £60 at 30 September Year 7, was traded in for £10 on 1 October Year 7, for another costing £250; the balance of the purchase price was covered by a hire purchase transaction involving 24 monthly payments of £12 commencing 1 November Year 7. All instalments have been paid as they became due on the first day of each month.
3. The loan account shown on 30 September Year 5 has been paid off.
4. A fire destroyed some work in progress which was still at the risk of the builder; this was not adequately covered by insurance, and the resultant loss was estimated to have been £400.
5. Early in Year 6 AH sold his house and furniture for £6,000 and went to live with his married daughter. The money received has been merged into the business funds.
6. During the period under consideration, AH has paid three income tax assessments from the firm's bank account, amounting in all to £1,070.

You are required to calculate as accurately as possible the trading profit of the business of AH for the period from 1 October Year 5 to 30 September Year 8, clearly distinguishing the normal trading profit from the exceptional or non-trading items.

(I.C.W.A.)

Suggested Solution:

Calculation of Profit for the trading period commencing 1 October Year 5 to 30 September Year 8

Net Assets at 30 September Year 8

Plant		£1,750	
Motor Vehicles		600	
Stock		1,455	
Work-in-Progress	£5,150		
Less: Deposits	710		
		4,440	
Debtors		205	
Cash		1,085	
		£9,535	
Less: Trade Creditors	508		
Hire Purchase Creditor (Note 1)	130		
Accrued Hire Purchase Interest (Note 2)	2		
		640	
			£8,895
Add: Drawings			
Cash (£15 per week for 3 years)		2,340	
Income Tax Payments		1,070	
			3,410
			12,305
Less: Capital introduced during period			
Proceeds from sale of house and furniture			6,000
			6,305
Less: Net Assets at 30 September Year 5			4,000
Profit for 3 years ended 30 September Year 8			£2,305

Calculation of Profit before charging exceptional non-trading items

Profit for 3 years ended 30 Sept. Year 8 as shown above		£2,305
Add: Loss caused through fire	£400	
Loss on sale of cement mixer	50	
		450
Profit for 3 years ended 30 September Year 8 before charging exceptional items		£2,755

Working Notes

1. *Calculation of Hire Purchase Creditor's balance*

Cost price of Cement Mixer	£250
Less: Deposit (Trade-in allowance on old cement mixer)	10
	£240

Balance repayable under H.P. Agreement (Principal)	£240
Less: 11 payments of Principal @ £10 each	110
Balance of Principal outstanding at 30 Sept. Year 8	£130

2. *Calculation of Interest due and unpaid at 30 September Year 8*

Balance of Interest under H.P. Agreement	£48

(H.P. price £288—Cost Price £240)
Taken on an average basis = *£2 per month*
Balance due and unpaid at 30 Sept. Year 8 = *£2*

9.3 SINGLE ENTRY ACCOUNTING SYSTEM WITH THE INTRODUCTION OF A CASH BOOK

It has been stated in an earlier section that the single entry system of accounting only involves the writing up of one book, viz. personal ledger. In practice it is found that this system, because of its limitations, is very rarely used as the businessman is usually anxious to ascertain more information about the detailed composition of his profit or loss. If a business, however small, is to be efficiently conducted, certain additional information must be known such as the gross profit percentage on sales, the various nominal expenses—wages and salaries, heat, light, rent, rates, and insurance. Previous years' figures for income and expenditure are also required for cost comparison, and to obtain these figures trading and profit and loss accounts have to be prepared. To do this the single entry records have to be converted to double entry. This is accomplished by introducing a cash book thus departing from the fundamental principle of single entry. By writing up a cash book it is possible to convert in total the single entry accounting system to double entry. This technique can be acquired by studying the illustrations following this section. Possibly the best form of cash book to use in this system is a tabular one with analysis columns on the debit side for discount allowed, cash sales, amounts received from debtors, and sundry income, and on the credit side columns for discount received, payments to creditors, cash purchases, and the nominal expenses which recur frequently over the trading period. With the cash book so analysed the amounts are in a readily available form to be incorporated in the working notes which are compiled before preparing the final accounts.

In conclusion, the requirements to convert single entry records to double entry are as undernoted:

(a) Statement of Affairs or Balance Sheet at the start of the trading period.
(b) Statement of Affairs or Balance Sheet at the end of the trading period.
(c) Summary of the receipts and payments during the period.

In theoretical problems adequate information will be given to enable one to compile the above statements, if necessary, which should be shown as working notes before attempting to prepare the Trading and Profit and Loss Accounts and Balance Sheet.

This practical question illustrates the technique adopted to solve a problem where a cash book has been introduced to a single entry accounting system.

Question

B, a retailer, keeps his books on an incomplete records system. The summary of his cash book transactions for the year ended 31 December Year 8 is as follows:

SUMMARY OF CASH BOOK

Balance in Bank—1 Jan. Year 8	£300	Payments to Creditors	£11,000
Cash Sales	10,000	Cash Purchases	500
Received from Debtors	5,000	Electricity	50
		Rent and Rates	100
		Wages	2,000
		Advertising	10
		General Expenses	40
		Balance in Bank—31 Dec. Year 8	1,600
	£15,300		£15,300

B submits the following list of his assets and liabilities:

	1 Jan. Year 8	31 Dec. Year 8
Stock	£1,500	£1,750
Motor Van	800	700
Debtors	400	900
Creditors	1,400	1,600
Accrued Charge—Wages	50	30
Prepaid Charge—Rates	20	30

Discount received from creditors amounted to £100. B took goods valued at cost £200 for his own use during the year.

You are required to prepare from the above information a Trading and Profit and Loss Account for year ended 31 December Year 8, and a Balance Sheet as at that date.

Suggested Solution:

Trading Account for Year ended 31 December Year 8

Purchases (Note (*a*))	£11,600		Sales (Note (*a*))		£15,500
Add: Stock at 1 Jan.					
Year 8	1,500				
	———				
	13,100				
Less: Stock at 31 Dec.					
Year 8	1,750				
	———	£11,350			
Gross Profit for Year		4,150			
		———			———
		£15,500			£15,500

Profit and Loss Account for Year ended 31 December Year 8

Wages (Note (*a*))	£1,980	Gross Profit	£4,150
Rent and Rates (Note (*a*))	90	Discount received	100
Electricity	50		
Advertising	10		
General Expenses	40		
Depreciation on Motor Van			
(Note (*c*))	100		
Profit for Year	1,980		
	———		———
	£4,250		£4,250

Balance Sheet as at 31 December Year 8

Capital Account				*Fixed Asset*		
As at 1 Jan. Year 8				Motor Van	£800	
(Note (*d*))	£1,570			*Less:* Depreciation	100	
Add: Profit for Year	1,980				———	£700
	———					
	3,550			*Current Assets*		
Less: Drawings (Goods				Stock	1,750	
for own use) (Note (*e*))	200			Debtors	900	
	———	£3,350		Prepaid Charge	30	
				Bank	1,600	
Current Liabilities					———	4,280
Creditors	1,600					
Accrued Charge	30					
	———	1,630				
		———				———
		£4,980				£4,980

Additional Notes

(*a*) *Calculation of Purchases, Sales, Rent and Rates, and Wages for Year*

		Purchases	Sales	Rent and Rates	Wages
Per Cash Book Summary		£11,000⎫ 500⎭	£5,000⎫ 10,000⎭	£100	£2,000
Add: Creditors and Accrued Charge at 31 Dec. Year 8		1,600			30
Prepayment at 1 Jan. Year 8				20	
Debtors at 31 Dec. Year 8			900		
Discount received		100			
		£13,200	£15,900	£120	£2,030
Less: Creditors and Accrued Charge at 1 Jan. Year 8	£1,400				50
Prepayment at 31 Dec. Year 8				30	
Debtors at 1 Jan. Year 8			400		
Goods taken by B for own use	200	1,600			
		£11,600	£15,500	£90	£1,980

The above presentation is in columnar form but this information may be shown in ledger form.

(b) *Alternative Presentation in Ledger Form*

Dr.		*Creditors' Control Account*	Cr.
Payments to Creditors	£11,000	Balance 1 Jan.	£1,400
Cash Purchases	500	Drawings (Goods for own	
Discount Received	100	use)	200
Balance—31 Dec.	1,600	Purchases	11,600
	£13,200		£13,200

The purchases figure of £11,600 is calculated by totalling the debit entries (£13,200) and deducting the total of the two credit entries (£1,600). The above account is similar in format to the normal Creditors' Control Account and is useful, in this instance, to calculate the purchases amount for the year. For the purposes of simplicity cash purchases have been included in the Creditors' Control Account.

		Debtors' Control Account	
Balance 1 Jan.	£400	Received from Debtors	£5,000
Sales	15,500	Cash Sales	10,000
		Balance 31 Dec.	900
	£15,900		£15,900

In the same way the sales figure £15,500 is calculated by totalling the credit entries (£15,900) and subtracting the debit entry (£400). The layout is similar to a Debtors' Control Account and enables the figures for sales to be calculated. Cash Sales, in this example, have been included in the Debtors' Control Account.

		Rent and Rates Account	
Balance 1 Jan.	£20	Balance 31 Dec.	£30
Paid during year	100	Profit and Loss	90
	£120		£120

The calculation of the rent and rates charge for the year can also be shown in ledger form bringing out the amount to be transferred to Profit and Loss Account.

Dr.		*Wages Account*	Cr.
Paid during year	£2,000	Balance 1 Jan.	£50
Balance 31 Dec.	30	Profit and Loss	1,980
	£2,030		£2,030

The calculation of wages charge for year is illustrated in ledger form.

(c) *Calculation of Depreciation Written Off Motor Van*

Valuation of Motor Van at 1 Jan.	£800
Less: Valuation of Motor Van at 31 Dec.	700
	£100

(d) *Calculation of Net Assets as at 1 January Year 8*

Assets

Motor Van		£800
Stock		1,500
Debtors		400
Prepaid Charge		20
Bank		300
		£3,020
Less: Liabilities		
Creditors	£1,400	
Accrued Charge	50	
		1,450
		£1,570

B's Capital = Net Assets = £1,570

(e) *Goods taken for B's own use.* The goods taken for B's own use have been valued at cost price and therefore the amount has been adjusted in the purchases for the year. It is usual to value this item at cost price.

Opposite is an examination problem illustrating the technique of preparing final accounts from incomplete records. The working notes have been shown in some detail to fully explain the method adopted to solve the question.

Question

R. Oldcastle is in business as a retailer and supplies to you the following particulars:

SUMMARY OF CASH BOOK

Receipts

Payments by debtors	£2,290
Cash Sales	3,110
Shop Fittings sold (valued at 31 Dec. Year 7 at £40)	30
Loan from W. Manor (interest free)	100
Withdrawn from Deposit Account	150
Interest on Deposit Account	3

Payments

Lodged in Current Account	3,600
Purchases	870
Salaries	600
Rent, Rates, and Insurance	110
Electricity	50
Travelling Expenses	85
Legal Expenses	36
Sundry Expenses	193
Private expenses of proprietor	130

Cheque payments were made as follows:

Purchase of new shop fittings	100
Lodged in Deposit Account	500
Purchases	3,200
Motor Van insurance	30
Fire insurance in respect of shop stock	17
Private income tax	100
Shop fittings £150, *less* allowed on trade in of old fittings exchanged valued at £50 at 31 Dec. Year 7	120

You are given the undernoted information:

1. R. Oldcastle has drawn a salary of £250 during the year. This has been included in the salaries amount.
2. The balance on the Deposit Account at 31 December Year 7 amounted to £350.
3. The balance in bank on Current Account and cash in hand on 31 December Year 7 amounted to £505 and £20 respectively.
4. Goods taken at cost price for private purposes by the proprietor during the year amounted to £100. It was also agreed that one-fifth of rent, rates, and insurance and electricity charges should be charged to the proprietor.

5. Fire Insurance on stock to be prepaid by £5 at 31 December Year 8.

6. Debtors at 31 December Year 7 were £800 and at 31 December Year 8 £815, but included in the latter figure are debts amounting to £20 which were considered to be bad.

7. A motor van was purchased during the year for £300 less £90 in respect of an old one valued at 31 December Year 7 at £100. Oldcastle had paid a deposit of £40 out of his own pocket, failing to enter the transaction in his books, the balance remaining unpaid at 31 December Year 8.

8. Accrue £20 for travelling expenses at 31 December Year 8.

9. Depreciation has to be written off the motor van at the rate of 20% per annum.

10. The following valuations were made:

	31 Dec. Year 7	31 Dec. Year 8
Shop Fittings	£360	£500
Stocks	820	965
Creditors for purchasers	700	720

You are required to prepare Trading and Profit and Loss Accounts for year ended 31 December Year 8 and a Balance Sheet as at that date.

Suggested Solution:

R. OLDCASTLE

Trading Account for Year ended 31 December Year 8

Purchases (Note (b))	£3,990		Sales (Note (b))	£5,415
Add: Stock 1 Jan. Year 8	820			
	4,810			
Less: Stock 31 Dec. Year 8	965			
		£3,845		
Gross Profit		1,570		
		£5,415		£5,415

Profit and Loss Account for Year ended 31 December Year 8

Salaries (Note (*f*))		£350	Gross Profit	£1,570
Electricity (Note (*b*))		40	Interest on Deposit Account	3
Rent, Rates, and Insurance (Note (*b*))		100		
Travelling Expenses (Note (*b*))		105		
Legal Expenses		36		
Bad Debt (Note (*e*))		20		
Motor Insurance		30		
Sundry Expenses		193		
Loss on sale of motor van (Note (*c*))		10		
Loss on sale of shop fittings (Note (*c*))		30		
Depreciation—				
Motor Van (Note (*c*))	£60			
Shop Fittings (Note (*c*))	20			
	—	80		
Profit for Year		579		
		£1,573		£1,573

Balance Sheet as at 31 December Year 8

Capital				*Fixed Assets*		
As at 1 Jan. Year 8				Motor Van: (Note (*c*))		
(Note (*h*))	£2,255			As at 1 Jan. Year 8	£100	
Add: Profit for Year	579			*Less:* Proceeds of Sale £90		
	———			Loss on Sale 10		
	2,834				— 100	
Less: Drawings (Note (*d*))	572				═══	
	———	£2,262		Purchased during year	300	
				Less: Depreciation	60	
Interest free loan from					—	£240
W. Manor		100		Shop Fittings: (Note (*c*))		
				As at 1 Jan. Year 8	360	
Current Liabilities				*Less:* Proceeds of sale 60		
Creditors	720			Loss on Sale 30		
Amount due on Motor					— 90	
Van (Note (*g*))	170				———	
Accrued Charge	20				270	
	—	910		*Add:* Purchased during		
				year	250	
					———	
					520	
				Less: Depreciation	20	
					—	500
						———
						740
				Current Assets		
				Stock	965	
				Debtors (Note (*e*))	795	
				Prepaid Charge	5	
				Bank Deposit Account		
				(Note (*a*))	700	
				Bank Current Account		
				(Note (*a*))	38	
				Cash on Hand		
				(Note (*a*))	29	
					—	2,532
		———				———
		£3,272				£3,272
		═══				═══

Additional Notes

(*a*) *Calculation of Cash and Bank Balances*

	Cash Account	Current Account	Deposit Account
As at 31 Dec. Year 7	£20	£505	£350
Add: Lodged during year		3,600	500
Cash received	5,683		
	5,703	4,105	850
Less: Withdrawn			150
Cash Paid	5,674	4,067	
	£29	£38	£700

(b)

	Sales		Purchases		Electricity		Rent, Rates, and Insurance		Travelling Expenses
Paid by Debtors	2,290								
Cash Sales and Purchases	3,110		870						85
Cash Payments					50		110		
Bank Payments			3,200				17		
Debtors and Creditors at 31 Dec. Year 8	815		720						20
Accrued at 31 Dec. Year 8					—				
	6,215		4,790		50		127		105
Less: Debtors and Creditors at 31 Dec. Year 7	800	700							
Goods taken for private use		100	800						
Proportion of expenses charged to proprietor				$(\frac{1}{5} \times £50)$ 10		$(\frac{1}{5} \times £110)$ 22			
Prepaid at 31 Dec. Year 8						5			
							27		
	£5,415		£3,990		£40		£100		£105

(c) Depreciation on Motor Van and Shop Fittings

		Motor Van		Shop Fittings
As at 31 Dec. Year 7		£100		£360
Less: Sold during year	£90		(30 + 30) £60	
Loss on sale	10		(10 + 20) 30	
	—	100	—	90
				270
Purchased during year		300 (100 + 150)		250
				520
Less: Depreciation	(20%)	60		20
Balance as at 31 Dec. Year 8		£240		£500

(d) Personal Drawings

Salary		£250
Cash Expenses		130
Income Tax		100
Goods taken for own use		100
Proportion of Expenses		
re Electricity	£10	
Rent, Rates, and Insurance	22	
	—	32
		612
Less: Deposit paid on Motor Van not recorded		40
		£572

(e) Debtors

As at 31 Dec. Year 8	£815
Less: Bad Debts	20
	£795

(f) Salaries

Per Cash Account	£600
Less: Salary of proprietor	250
	£350

(g) *Amount Due on Motor Van*

Purchase price		£300
Less: Deposit paid by proprietor	£40	
Trade-in allowance on old van	90	
	—	130
		£170

(h) *Calculation of Capital at 1 January Year 8*

Assets

Shop Fittings	£360	
Motor Van	100	
Stock	820	
Debtors	800	
Bank—Deposit Account	350	
Current Account	505	
Cash	20	
	£2,955	
Less: Creditors	700	
	£2,255	

Examination Questions

Question 1

George Humphrey keeps his books on a Single Entry basis and submits the following Statement of his Affairs at 31 December Year 3.

Statement of Affairs as at 31 December Year 3

Liabilities		Assets	
Capital	£7,866	Fixtures	£600
Sundry Creditors	807	Stock	3,962
		Sundry Debtors	3,220
		Cash at Bank	891
	£8,673		£8,673

His Statement of Affairs at 31 December Year 2, showed his Capital as £6,751

He requests you to calculate his profit for the year ended 31 December Year 3, and to redraft the Statement of Affairs given above.

During the year Humphrey withdrew £75 a month from the business and also took £100 worth of Stock for his private use. He received during the year a legacy of £600 and he sold his private car for £210; both these amounts were paid into the business.

Fixtures are to be depreciated by 10% and a provision of 5% is to be made for bad and doubtful debts.

(L. Ch. of C.)

Question 2

On 1 January Year 5 Jack won £6,000 and decided to buy a Freehold Garage with Car Hire Business. The consideration was £6,500 which included in addition to legal costs of £174, fittings and equipment £190, three private cars valued at £1,380, debtors £90, petrol and spares £298, licences and insurances prepaid £62, less electricity due £28. The balance of £500 was loaned to Jack by his wife.

Only memorandum records are kept and the following facts are ascertained:

1. Jack buys from a dealer for his own personal use, a car costing £520 and uses petrol costing £40.
2. One of the cars originally valued at £350 was sold for £375 and a new car purchased for £580.
3. Personal drawings amounted to £420.
4. Jack has repaid £300 to his wife.
5. Additional equipment was purchased costing £165.
6. Of Debtors taken over, only £60 proved to be collectable and further Bad Debts of £45 were incurred and written off during the year.
7. During the year Jack started a Travel Agency and he had collected deposits in respect of future bookings amounting to £150 of which £130 had been forwarded to his Principals.

At the end of the year Cash in Hand was £267, Creditors for Spares and Petrol £66, Prepayment £78, Petrol and Spares £193, Debtors £57. Depreciation at the rate of 20% is to be provided on all vehicles in use at the end of the year and at the rate of 15% on Fittings and Equipment.

You are required to prepare:

(a) A calculation of trading results for the year.
(b) A Balance Sheet of the Business as at 31 December Year 5.

                                                        (I.C.W.A.)

Question 3

J.G., a trader, pays all his business takings into his bank account. All business payments are made by cheque. The following is a summary of his Bank Account for Year 3:

Bank Summary

Balance 31 Dec. Year 2	£240	Trade Creditors	£12,400
Received from Debtors for		General Expenses	1,262
goods	15,780	Rent	150
		Drawings	1,800
		Balance 31 Dec. Year 3	408
	£16,020		£16,020

The following information is obtained from the Books:

	31 December Year 2	31 December Year 3
Debtors for goods sold	£950	£1,172
Trade Creditors	830	965
Creditors for General Expenses	70	410
Stock in Trade	1,020	924
Furniture and Fittings	200	180

Discounts allowed to customers during Year 3 amounted to £300. No discounts were received from suppliers.

Throughout Year 3, J.G., occupied a building at a rent of £200 a year. The building is divided equally between business and private occupation.

You are required (a) to show your calculation of the balance on J.G.'s Capital Account at 31 December Year 2, and (b) to prepare the Trading and Profit and Loss Account for Year 3 and Balance Sheet as on 31 December Year 3.
(C.I.S.)

Question 4

Michael Malone is a Sole Trader who does not keep his books on a full double-entry system. All his Sales and Purchases are on credit but he neither allows nor receives discount in respect of cash received or paid. An examination of his records reveals the following position:

	31 December Year 5	31 December Year 6
Stock	£1,240	£1,370
Debtors	5,990	6,380
Creditors	2,820	2,960
Office Furniture (Valuation)	400	470
Cash at Bank	940	?

During Year 6 his Sales amounted to £6,830 and his Purchases to £2,880. Cash received from Debtors during Year 6 was £6,440 and paid to Creditors £2,740. Malone does not keep any cash in his office but during Year 6 he withdrew from the bank a total of £2,400. Out of this he purchased new Office Furniture for £100 (included in the £470 figure at 31 December Year 6, given above), Wages £1,220, and General Expenses £280. The balance of the cash withdrawn was taken by Malone as drawings.

From the above you are required to:
(a) Calculate Malone's Capital at 31 December Year 5.
(b) Draw up a summary of his Cash Book for Year 6.
(c) Draw up his Trading and Profit and Loss Accounts for Year 6, together with a Balance Sheet as on 31 December Year 6.

(L. Ch. of C.)

Question 5

On 1 January Year 5, G. Green began trading as a Retailer and opened a banking account on that date into which he later paid all his takings periodically after making various payments in cash and retaining £5 for a cash float. These cash payments and all other transactions are entered in a diary but no other records are kept. From the diary you obtain the following summary of the transactions:

> Bank:
>> Encashed National Savings Certificates realizing £1,750
>> Paid (Jan. 1) six months rent in advance £130
>> Paid Insurance on Stock for year to 31 Dec. Year 5, £24
>> Purchased (Feb. 1) Motor Van cost £600
>> Paid for Stocks £864 after deducting £22 discount
>
> Cash:
>> Sales £1,086
>> Paid to Bank £870
>> Purchases for Stock £45
>> Personal Expenditure and Drawings £91
>> Sundry Expenditure £20

You also ascertain the following facts from Mr. Green:

> Stock at 31 Mar. Year 5, £407
> Debtors at 31 Mar. Year 5, £20
> Goods supplied but not paid for £200

At the start of business, Mr. Green brought Fixtures valued at £150 into the business. These are to be depreciated at 10% per annum of their value. The motor van is to be depreciated at 25% per annum of cost.

From the above summary, compile the Trading and Profit and Loss Account for the three months to 31 March Year 5, and a Balance Sheet as at that date.

(A.C.C.A.)

Question 6

You are asked to prepare a Trading and Profit and Loss Account (showing clearly the cost of goods sold) and a Balance Sheet in respect of a sole trader's business activities for Year 6. The following information is obtained from the trader and his business records:

	1 January Year 6	31 December Year 6
Shop Fittings (Purchased 1 Jan. Year 1) at cost (No items sold or scrapped during Year 6)	£8,400	£8,400
Shop Expenses in advance	200	250
Stock-in-Trade	5,600	6,250
Trade Creditors	4,230	4,470
Shop Expense Creditors	520	480
Trade Debtors	75	120
Cash at Bank as on bank statements	2,450	3,220
Cash in Hand	50	70
Cheques for trade goods drawn earlier, but not presented at 31 Dec. Year 6	—	320

	Bank Statement	Cash
Payments:		
Trade Goods	£20,980	£29,230
Shop Wages	—	3,780
Shop Expenses	1,220	3,140
Customers cheque dishonoured (subsequently honoured)	15	—
Shop Fittings (Purchased 1 Jan. Year 6)	1,400	—
Personal Cheques	945	
Receipts:		
Sales	1,120	60,130
Sweepstake Prize	250	
Cash banked	23,960	—

Goods taken for household use:
at selling price   £1,350 (Cost Price £1,100)
Depreciation rate on Shop Fittings—10% per annum on cost.

(C.I.S.)

Question 7

A. Brown is in business as a Retailer and the undernoted particulars are supplied in respect of his business:

Analysis of the Bank and Cash transactions for Year 7 shows:

Private Drawings	£310
Motor Van purchased £300, *less* allowance for old van, £80	220
Cash Sales and amounts received from Debtors	5,050
Motor Expenses	80
Sundry Expenses	75
Rent, Rates, and Insurance	132
Salaries of Sales Staff	1,020
Cash refund from Creditor	10
Bills Payable met when due	300
Payments to Creditors and Cash Purchases	2,800

	31 December Year 6	31 December Year 7
Motor Van	£90	See above
Fixtures and Fittings	500	500
Creditors for Goods Purchased	470	490
Cash on Hand	20	30
Bills Payable	180	160
Stock	800	790
Debtors	905	890
Bank Overdraft	198	105
Rent accrued	15	See below
Insurance prepaid	5	See below

Included in the Cash Purchases are Stationery £18 and Shop Fire Insurance Premium £25. All Bills transactions relate to goods for resale.

The following additional matters have to be taken into account at 31 December Year 7:

Bad Debts	£38
Rent accrued	20
Insurance Prepaid	6
Depreciation Motor Van 25%	
Depreciation on Fixtures and Fittings 5%	

You are required to prepare a Trading and Profit and Loss Account for Year 7 and a Balance Sheet at 31 December Year 7.

Index

Acceptor, 110
Accommodation Bills, 112–13
Accounting
  double entry, 1–28, 65, 136
    alternatives, 150
    basic principles, 4–6
    petty cash books, 60, 61
    proof by Trial Balances, 20
    role of Day Books, 11
  errors, 65–7, 128
  function in management, 2, 141
  meaning and purpose, 1
Accounting entries
  Accommodation Bills, 113
  accrued income, 40
  assets, 88–9, 92–6
  bad debts recovered, 44
  Bills of Exchange, 115–24
  control accounts, 133
  debits, 4, 9
  discounted Bills, 118–19
  fixed assets, 88–9, 92–6
  honoured Bills, 119–20
  petty cash books, 61–3, 64–5
  prepaid charges, 39
  prepaid income, 41
  procedures, 6
  provision for bad debts, 42–3
  renewal of Bills of Exchange, 117–18, 121–2
  stock accounts, 31
  transfer of balance to Profit and Loss Account, 32
Accounting personnel, 1, 67
Accounting records, 1–2
  flexibility, 2
  information required, 2
Accounts
  asset, 6, 81
  customers, 10
  Depreciation Fund Investment, 83

Accounts—(contd.)
  Depreciation Provision, 79, 80
  Discount Allowed, 16, 44–5
  Discount Received, 45–6
  Interest, 81
  ledger, 7–9, 26, 51
  liability, 6
  manufacturing, 141–9
  nominal, 7
  personal, 7
  Plant, 79
  Profit and Loss, 2, 3, 29–55, 144, 159, 164–5, 172, 173, 174
    bad debts, 41
    bad debts recovered, 44
    classification, 46–7
    depreciation charges, 83
    discount allowed, 44–5
    incomplete records, 151
    link with Balance Sheets, 3
    preparation, 31–2
    purpose, 31
    relation to Manufacturing Accounts, 141
    revenue expenditure, 101, 102
  Provision for Bad Debts, 42–4, 52
  purchases, 30, 151
  real, 7
  Rent, 38, 161, 172
  Reserve, 85
  stock, 31
  suppliers, 10
  Trading, 2, 3, 29–55, 144, 159, 164–5, 172, 173, 174
    incomplete records, 151
    link with Balance Sheets, 3
    period covered, 30
    preparation, 29–31
    relation to Manufacturing Accounts, 141
    revenue expenditure, 101, 102

Accrued charges, 37, 152
  on Balance Sheets, 38–9
Accrued income, 40–1
Actuarial tables, 81
Adjustment of Cash Book balances, 57–8
Administration, 46–7
Alteration of entries, 67
Amounts due, 2
Annuity system 81–3
Approximations of depreciation charges,
    83, 85
Asset Accounts, 6, 81
  capital expenditure, 101
Assets, 2, 3–4, 7, 32
  accounting entries, 88–9, 92–6
  as capital investments, 81
  capital expenditure, 101–8
  depreciation, 75–100
  deterioration, 75–6
  expenditure on acquisition, 102
  inadequacy, 76
  low-cost, 80, 88
  obsolescence, 76
  original cost, 76
  Plant Register, 88, 90–1
  provision for replacement, 83
  purchasing, 18
    accounting entries, 88–9
  relation to liabilities and capital, 4
  repair charges, 106–7
  replacement, 83, 88
  sale, 18
    accounting entries, 88–9
  service life, 75, 77
  trade-in values, 77
  wasting, 87
  writing off, 77, 78
  See also Fixed assets; Net assets

Bad debts, 41–4, 52, 102
  paid into Bank, 56
  provision for, 42–4
  recovered, 44
Bad Debts Recovered Accounts, 44
Balance Sheets, 2, 5–6, 25, 51, 166
  accrued charges, 38–9
  debtors, 43–4
  Discount Received Accounts, 45
  from incomplete records, 151, 152–7
  note of contingent liability, 115
  prepaid charges, 39–40

Balance Sheets—(contd.)
  presentation, 6
  purpose, 3–4
  See also Statements of Affairs
Balances (ledger accounts), 9
Bank Accounts, 5–6, 13
Bank balances, 2, 167, 172, 173
  interest debited, 57
  Statement of Affairs, 152
Bank charges, 57, 58
Bank Holidays, 113
Bank overdrafts, 3, 18, 58
Bank Reconciliation Statements, 56–9,
    69–70
  preparation, 57–8
  purposes, 56
Bank statements, 56–9
  agreement with Cash Book, 56
  reasons for not agreeing with Cash
    Books, 56–7
Banks
  cheques, 56, 57, 109, 115
  discounting bills, 111, 122
    accounting entries, 118–19
    contingent liability, 115
    procedure, 112
    subsequently dishonoured, 121
Bills of Exchange, 109–13
  Accommodation Bills, 112–13
  accounting entries, 115–24
  advantages, 111
  days of grace, 113
  definitions, 109, 110–11
  discounted, 111, 122
    accounting entries, 118–19
    contingent liability, 115
    procedure, 112
    subsequently dishonoured, 121
  dishonoured, 120, 121, 122
    charges incurred, 111–12, 116–17
    procedures, 111–12
  endorsed, 118, 119
  for obtaining credit, 111
  honoured, 116, 119–20, 122
  parties to, 110–11
  renewal
    accounting entries, 117–18, 121–2
    procedure, 112
  transferrable, 110, 111
Bills of Exchange Act (1882), 109, 113,
    115

Bills Payable, 110
Bills Payable books, 113, 114
Bills Receivable, 110
Bills Receivable books, 113, 114
Books of original entry, 13, 18
'By' (prefix to credit entries), 9

Capital, 3–4, 151, 173
  introduced, 152
  investing, 1, 81
  relation to assets and liabilities, 4
Capital Accounts, 32
Capital expenditure, 101–8
  distinguished from revenue expenditure, 102–3, 107–8
Carriage Inwards costs, 29
Cars. *See* Motor vehicles
Cash Accounts, 5, 13–16, 167, 173
Cash at bank, 2, 152
Cash Books, 13–18, 70–1, 129, 131, 133, 173
  adjustment of balances, 57–8
  agreement with bank statements, 56
  Bank Reconciliation statements, 56
  columnar, 18
  contra entries, 14, 138
  double entry principles, 13
  in single entry systems, 157–62
  incomplete records, 151
  reasons for not agreeing with bank statements, 56–7
  summary, 160
  tabular, 157–8
  three-column, 16–18, 27
  two-column, 13–15, 27
Cash Discounts, 44
Cash floats. *See* Imprest system
Cash in hand, 2, 152
Cashiers, 56
  See also Personnel
Charges
  accrued, 37, 152
  on Balance Sheets, 38–9
Cheques, 56, 57, 109, 115
  prepaid, 37, 39–40, 152
  time-lag to banking, 56
Cheques Act (1957), 109
Christmas Day, 113
Classification of accounts
  administration, 46–7
  finance, 46–7

Classification of accounts—*(contd.)*
  selling, 46–7
Cleaning materials, 60
Columnar Cash Books, 18
  See also Two-column Cash Books; Three-column Cash Books
Columnar Day Books, 13
Commission, 101
Companies Act (1948), 80, 115
Contingent liability, 115
Contra entries, 14, 138
Control Accounts, 134, 136
  accounting entries, 133
  comparison with Total Accounts, 133
  creditors, 137, 138
  debtors, 137, 138, 161
  distinction from Total Accounts, 136
  requirement for, 127
Cost statements, 2
Credit, 6, 10, 41
  Bills of Exchange, 111
Credit entries, 4
  use of 'By', 9
Credit notes, 10
Credit sales, 9
Creditors, 3
  Control Accounts, 137, 138, 161
  total balances, 128
Customers Accounts, 10

Day Books, 9–13, 26
  columnar, 13
  Purchases, 10–11, 18, 26
  Purchases Returns, 10–11, 18
  relation to double entry system, 11
  role in double entry accounting, 11
  Sales, 9–10, 11, 12, 18
  Sales Returns, 10, 11, 18
Days of Grace, 113
Debit entries, 4, 6
  use of 'To', 9
Debtors, 43–4, 52, 169
  Bills of Exchange, 111
  Control Accounts, 137, 138, 161
  promissory notes, 115
  total balances, 42, 128
  See also Bad debts; Provision for Bad Debts Accounts
Debts
  foreign, 111
  See also Bad debts

Departmental Accounts, 2
Depletion method, 87
Depreciation, 75–100, 169, 171
  annuity system, 81–3
  approximation of charges, 83, 85
  basic concepts, 75
  by fixed percentage, 79
  depletion method, 87
  determining charges, 76–7
  fixed instalment method, 77–9
  hourly rates, 88
  insurance policy method, 85–7
  machine hour system, 88
  need for constant review of policies, 76
  of assets, 75–100
  of fixtures, 174
  reducing balance method, 79–80, 96, 98
  replacement and renewals basis, 88
  revaluation method, 80–1
  Sinking Fund method, 83–5
  through deterioration, 75–6
  through inadequacy, 76
  through obsolescence, 76
Depreciation Accounts, 83–5
Depreciation charges, 83
Depreciation Fund Accounts, 87
Depreciation Fund Investment Accounts, 83
Depreciation Provision Accounts, 79, 80
Deterioration of assets, 75–6
Discount Allowed Accounts, 16, 44–5
Discount Received Accounts, 45–6
  on Balance Sheets, 45
Discounting
  Bills of Exchange, 111, 122
    accounting entries, 118–19
    contingent liability, 115
    procedure, 112
    subsequently dishonoured, 121
Discounts, 16, 172
  customers, 16, 44–5
  trade, 12, 16, 45–6
Dishonoured bills, 120, 121, 122
  charges incurred, 111–12, 116–17
  procedure, 111–12
Double entry accounting, 1–28, 65, 136
  alternatives to, 150
  basic principles, 4–6
  Cash Books, 13

Double entry accounting—(contd.)
  Petty Cash Books, 60, 61
  proof by Trial Balances, 20
  role of Day Books, 11
Doubtful debts. See Bad debts
Drawee, 109, 110
Drawer, 109, 110
Drawings, 152, 154, 169

Endorsed bills, 118, 119
Endorser, 111
Endowment policies, 86–7
Equity, 3
Erasing entries, 67
Errors, 65–7, 128
  compensating, 66
  correction, 18, 72, 73, 127
  masked by Trial Balances, 20
  of commission, 66
  of omission, 66
  of original entry, 65–6
  of principle, 65
  rectifying, 66–9
Expense Accounts
  adjustment for prepaid charges, 39
  revenue expenditure, 101
Expenses, 7, 31
  travelling, 48, 60

Factory costs, 141, 142
Factory costs of finished goods, 141, 142–3
Final Accounts, 3
Finance, 46–7
Financial information, 1
Financial statements, 2–3
Finished goods, 143
Fittings, 7
Fixed assets, 18, 152
  accounting entries, 88–9, 92–6
  See also Assets; Net assets
Fixed instalment method, 77–9
Fixtures, 174
Floats. See Imprest system
Folios, 8–9
Foreign Bills, 109
Foreign debts, 111
Furniture, 7

Good Friday, 113
Gross losses, 30
  See also Losses

Gross profits, 29
  See also Profits

Holder, 111
Holder in due course, 111
Honoured bills, 116, 119–20, 122
Hourly rates of depreciation, 88

Impersonal ledgers, 7, 63
  Discount Allowed Accounts, 16
  petty cash accounts, 60
Imprest system, 63–5, 71–2
Inadequacy of assets, 76
Income
  accrued, 40–1
  prepaid, 40–1
Incomplete records, 1, 150–75
  cash books, 151
  single entry systems, 150–7
  single entry systems with cash book,
    157–62
Information from accounts, 2
Inland Bills, 109
Insolvency, 41
Instalments. *See* Fixed instalment
  method
Insurance policies, 85–7
Insurance premiums, 39
Interest
  debited by Bank, 57
  on investments, 81, 83–5
Interest Accounts, 81
Inventory procedures, 80
Investments, 86, 154
  dividends, 56
  interest, 81, 83–5
  to provide replacement funds, 83

Journal entries, 19
  accrued charges, 37
  totalling, 20
Journals, 18–20, 72–3
  rulings, 19
  to rectify errors, 67–9

Leases, 81–3
Ledger Accounts, 7–9, 26, 51
  balancing, 9
  division, 8
  transfers, 18
  writing up, 8–9

Ledgers
  self-balancing, 127–31
  subdivision, 134, 135
Legal fees, 102
Liabilities, 3–4, 32
  relation to assets and capital, 4
Liability Accounts, 6
Loan accounts, 5
Loans, 3, 7
Losses, 7, 31
  assessment, 1
  See also Gross losses
Low-cost assets, 80, 88

Machine hour system, 88
Machinery, 7
  depreciation, 88
  See also Plant
Management, 3
Management function of accounting, 2,
  141
Manufacturing Accounts, 141–9
Mines, 87
Mortgages, 3
Motor vehicles, 7, 72

Negotiable instruments, 110
Net assets, 151
  See also Assets; Gross assets
Nominal Accounts, 7
Nominal ledgers, 7
Notary Public, 112

Obsolescence of assets, 76
Original entry, 13, 18
  errors of, 65–6
Overdrafts. *See* Bank overdrafts

Payee, 110–11
Period of accounts, 30
Personal Accounts, 7
Personnel, 1, 67
  See also Cashiers
Petty Cash Books, 60–5, 71–2
  accounting entries, 61–3, 64–5
  double entry accounting, 60, 61
  imprest system, 63–5, 71–2
Plant, 3, 7
  See also Machinery
Plant Accounts, 79
Plant maintenance, 106–7, 142

Plant Register, 78, 88, 90–1
Postage, 60
Posting
  errors, 65
  procedures, 6
  referencing, 9
Prepaid charges, 37, 152
  adjustment in Expense Accounts, 39
  on Balance Sheets, 39–40
Prepaid income, 40–1
Presentation of balance sheets, 6
Prime costs, 141, 142
Prime entry. *See* Original entry
Profit and Loss Accounts, 2, 3, 29–55, 144, 159, 164–5, 172, 173, 174
  bad debts, 41
  bad debts recovered, 44
  classification of accounts, 46–7
  depreciation charges, 83
  discount allowed, 44–5
  incomplete records, 151
  link with Balance Sheets, 3
  preparation, 31–2
  purpose, 31
  relation to Manufacturing Accounts, 141
  revenue expenditure, 101, 102
Profits, 31, 171
  assessment, 1
  See also Gross profits
Promissory Notes, 109, 113, 115
Property, 3, 7
Protest, 112
Provision for Bad Debts Accounts, 42–4, 52
Purchases, 2
Purchases Accounts, 30
  incomplete records, 151
Purchases Day Books, 10–11, 18
  rulings, 26
Purchases Ledger Total Accounts, 128
Purchases Ledgers, 7, 63, 127, 129
  construction of Total Accounts, 129–30
  Control Accounts, 133, 136, 137, 139–40
  subdivision, 134, 135
Purchases Returns Accounts, 10
Purchases Returns Day Books, 10–11, 18

Quarries, 87

Rates, 2
Rates Accounts, 161
Raw material stocks, 142, 143
Real Accounts, 7
Records, 1–2
Rectifying errors, 66–9
Reducing balance method, 79–80, 96, 98
Referencing postings, 9
Renewal of Bills of Exchange
  accounting entries, 117–18, 121–2
  procedure, 112
Rent Accounts, 38, 161, 172
Rents, 2
Repairs to buildings, 106–7
Repairs to plant, 106–7, 142
Replacement of assets, 83, 88
Reserve Accounts, 85
Residual values of assets, 76, 77
  determination of, 77
Revaluation method, 80–1
Revenue expenditure, 101–8
  distinguished from capital expenditure, 102–3, 107–8
Revenue expenses, 2

Salaries, 169
  of salesmen, 48
  See also Wages
Sale of assets, 18
Sales, 2
Sales Day Books, 9–10, 11, 18
  trade discounts, 12
Sales Ledger Total Accounts, 129–30
Sales Ledgers, 7, 127
  construction of Total Accounts, 131–2
  Control Accounts, 133, 136, 137, 139–40
  subdivision, 134, 135
  trade discounts, 12
Sales Returns Day Books, 10, 11, 18
Salesmen's salaries, 48
Self-balancing ledgers, 127–31
Selling, 46–7
Service life of assets, 77
Single entry accounting systems, 150–7 170
  with cash book, 157–62
Sinking Fund method, 83–5
Statements of Affairs, 151, 152–7, 158, 170
  See also Balance Sheets

Stationery charges, 60
Stock Accounts, 31
Stock valuation, 152
Stocks, 3, 29
    finished goods, 143
    raw materials, 143
'Straight line' method. *See* Fixed
    instalment method
Subdivision of ledgers, 134, 135
Sunday, 113
Supplies Accounts, 10
Surrender values, 86
Suspense Accounts, 37
    to rectify errors, 66

Tabular Cash Books, 157–8
Three-column Cash Books, 16–18, 27
    See also Columnar Cash Books; Two-
    column Cash Books
'To' (prefix to debit entries), 9
Tools, 80, 81
Total Accounts, 128–31
    comparison with Control Accounts,
    133
    construction, 129
    distinction from Control Accounts,
    136
    for subdivided ledgers, 134
Trade discounts, 12, 16, 45–6
Trade-in values, 77
Trading Accounts, 2, 3, 29–55, 144, 159,
    164–5, 172, 173, 174

Trading accounts—(*contd.*)
    incomplete records, 151
    link with Balance Sheets, 3
    period covered, 30
    preparation, 29–31
    relation to Manufacturing Accounts,
    141
    revenue expenditure, 101, 102
Transfers of Bills of Exchange, 110, 111
Transfers between accounts, 18, 20
Travelling expenses, 48, 60
Trial Balances, 20–5, 28, 48, 137
    failure to balance, 66, 67, 73
    masking errors, 20
    possibility of errors, 65–6
    proof of double-entry accounting, 20
    similarity to self-balancing ledgers,
    127
Two-column Cash Books, 13–15, 27
    See also Columnar Cash Books;
    Three-column Cash Books

Unexpired charges. *See* Prepaid charges

Wages, 2, 142, 161
    in Trading Accounts, 29
    See also Salaries
Wages Accounts, 37
Wasting assets, 87
Wear and tear. *See* Deterioration of
    assets
Writing-off assets, 77, 78
Writing up ledger accounts, 8–9